RIO DE JANEIRO

Ricardo Boechat

COPACABANA

A Hotel and its History

PALACE

PHOTOGRAPHS BY *Sergio Pagano*

Publisher
Alexandre Dórea Ribeiro

Executive Editor
Adriana Amback

Design
Victor Burton

Design Assistants
Adriana Moreno
Miriam Lerner
Raphaella Lemos

Photographs
Sergio Pagano

Director of Photography
Sergio Pagano

Research Coordinator
Hélio Kaltman

Image Research
Filomena Chiaradia

Text Research
Ana Reis
Andrea Santos de Oliveira
Carin Blanco V. Scarpa

Translation
Stuart Birkinshaw

English Language Consultants
Elizabeth Wynn-Jones
Jennifer Lynes

Production
Victor Burton Design
Estúdio DBA

Photolithography
Mergulhar Serviços Editoriais

Printed by
Gráfica Melhoramentos

CONTENTS

Preface

Maneco Müller (Jacinto de Thormes)

The Guinle family's considerable contribution to the style and history of the city of Rio is the subject of this volume by journalist Ricardo Boechat; as a preamble, it might be appropriate to describe the city before the advent of the Copacabana Palace.

The family's first hotel arose on Avenida Central (today's Avenida Rio Branco), soon after the city emerged from extensive rebuilding. Paris was the idea. Paris in the tropics. The Municipal Theatre, the School of Fine Arts, the headquarters of large corporations ... all were clearly copycat architecture. Even the stones for the sidewalks came from Europe. Rio fancied itself the Champs Elysées, and the worst of it was that the city was turned backside foremost: facing away from the sea. The people were in São Cristóvão, Tijuca, Botafogo, Laranjeiras. Hidden away, pretending they were somewhere else. Take, as an example, the Catete Palace, built for the Baron of Nova Friburgo: its windows faced the street; Guanabara Bay and the Sugar Loaf were at the rear of the house and completely ignored.

The lifestyle of the *carioca*, as the native of Rio is known, only changed after the construction of a tunnel leading to the beaches. Hitherto, the beach had not been part of Rio; it might, perhaps, have had potential, in the distant future, as a resort. But only maybe.

To this day, visitors have difficulty grasping the concept of a metropolis, former capital of the Republic, located right on the beach. The renowned Portuguese writer José Saramago once said that he couldn't quite take Rio seriously as a city. São Paulo, sure, but not Rio. And I remember the stupefaction of prince and playboy Ali Khan when his friends Lurdes and Álvaro Catão bought a house on Arpoador beach. Incredulous, he wondered whether they intended to stay at the seaside "through all the seasons," saying jokingly that "this isn't real life."

My personal bias is apparent, of course, because I have been defending the beach all my life. Like the Copa, I too am celebrating my 75th birthday. I was born on Avenida Atlântica, at the home of my grandfather. I must concede, however, that after its latest revamp, the hotel is in better shape than I am.

You will find this a good read, full of memories not listed in the archives, about a hotel that started out with European aspirations – Nice or Cannes – and which ended up as *carioca* as its setting. The story illustrates how the incredible landscape, the ozone and the waves melded with the gentlemanly ambitions of Otávio Guinle, his amiable formality and incomparable service. Tales strange but true abound, too – a famous ballet dancer who snatched the conductor's baton and proceeded to conduct and dance simultaneously; the President of the Republic who was shot in his suite by his mistress ... Ricardo Boechat, one of the best journalists I have ever encountered, relates it all in his clear, crisp style.

The sheer volume of information and the grandeur of so much of it explain why the "old Copa" is a part of Rio's history and even of its geography. After all, the hotel put the beach on the map and not the other way around. Stories of difficult and sad moments in the Copa's history, such as the terrible fire and the hotel's near bankruptcy, are not spared either.

You will put this book down feeling reassured that the new proprietors, who are responsible for so many international success stories, will maintain the traditions and style of the Copacabana Palace while keeping pace with the tempo of our modern times.

Happy reading.

Sergio Pagano

The Palace by the Sea

Variable

COPACABANA PALACE HOTEL
COPACABANA PALACE
·RIO DE JANEIRO·

PALACE HOTEL

COPACABANA
PALACE
RIO DE JANEIRO

Chapter One

A Tunnel to the Sea

The First Bather

When the Copacabana Palace first opened its doors in the winter of 1923, the view from its verandahs revealed the luminous blue of the sea and the endless, immaculate whiteness of the sand. A few dwellings and some charming summer homes dotted the landscape, and the fishermen beached their canoes in this setting made magical by the sun and the infinite ocean. Copacabana was a distant paradise in the urban life of Rio de Janeiro at this time, one which trams had only reached three decades before, at the close of the previous century. Hitherto, the prospect of a dip in the sea was not enough to lure people to Copacabana – in fact, bathing in the sea was not a habit among Rio's élite, while the poor preferred the Bay of Guanabara to the open sea. So bizarre did the rich consider the habit of bathing oneself in the ocean and stretching out on the sand that they claim a foreign tourist was Rio's first famous beach-goer. 1886 saw the arrival of the steamship *Cotopaxi*, whose passenger Sarah Bernhardt was to star at the Teatro São Pedro in *Froufrou* and *The Lady of the Camellias*. The French actress was greeted at the quayside by a crowd of three thousand admirers; days later she would shock the entire Court with the bathing attire she wore while sitting for hours in the sun, contemplating the horizon, in far-away Copacabana. Worse still, she went for a dip in the water after seven o'clock in the morning, entirely unacceptable behaviour for the times. In a letter to her friend R. Ponchon, she justified her outrageous gesture: "While the country is extraordinary, the climate is terrible, the heat extreme and the humidity frightful." Until recently, society had feared the combination of sun and sea. Sea bathing was an exclusively therapeutic activity, never practiced much later than dawn. Sunbathing was considered noxious to one's health; furthermore, the élite cultivated the whiteness of their skin to set themselves apart from the darker, poorer people. The authorities viewed bathing in the sea as a near mortal sin, unless it had been prescribed by a doctor. In 1917, Mayor Amaro Cavalcanti issued decree 1143, establishing hours and codes of behaviour for the practice of sea bathing in Leme and Copacabana. In summertime, bathing in the sea was permitted during two sessions: from five to eight o'clock in the morning and then from five to seven o'clock in the evening, with an extra hour being permitted on Sundays and public holidays. Bathers were required to "use appropriate clothing, observing the necessary decency and decorum;" additionally, "any noise or shouting on the beach or in the sea" was expressly forbidden. Non-compliance with any of the eight articles of the decree resulted in a fine of 20 thousand réis – or five days in the clink. Thirty years before Amaro Cavalcanti's decree, the behaviour of Sarah Bernhardt, whose notoriety granted her a measure of immunity from local criticism, planted the tiny, timid seeds of a change in style. Little by little, people became used to the pleasures of going to the beach – of salt water, of playing and resting on the beach. Thus, the people of Rio began to establish what endures to this day as their most characteristic and democratic habit. Sarah Bernhardt's scandalous instincts were not limited to the beach. In another letter to the same Monsieur Ponchon, she drew a cruel caricature of the Brazilian aristocracy; even the Emperor Dom Pedro II was not spared. She suspected that the Emperor was "too poor to afford a season ticket, as he arrives every night at the theatre in a carriage drawn by four breathless donkeys, who are quite as absurd as his bedraggled officers. These Brazilians seem to be perpetually at play. They play at building houses, at laying roads, at putting out fires,

A distant paradise, Copacabana had only been served by tram (above) for some thirty years. Actress Sarah Bernhardt (below and left, with her troupe in São Paulo) spent hours on Copacabana beach in bathing attire that outraged the conservative Brazilian Court

Mayor Pereira Passos' improvements changed the face of Rio. Over forty buildings were demolished on Rua da Carioca (top), and the stylishly elegant Avenida Central (above and below) was inaugurated

at being productive ..." In August of 1858, before Sarah Bernhardt's famous dips, Copacabana had already been the focus of general attention. A pair of whales was rumoured to be cavorting near the shore and a huge throng, which included Dom Pedro and Dona Teresa Cristina, had formed to watch; Copacabana's first major crowd had gathered. But the "giant mammals" could not be seen – if, indeed, they were in the vicinity at all. Even so, prompted by a collective curiosity which lasted a full three days, hundreds of people, many of them camping out, discovered the beauty of remote Copacabana. The origin of its name is as beautiful as the place. In Quíchua, an ancient American language which is still spoken in Peru, "Copa Caguana" means "luminous place." This is the name the Incas gave to the site where, on the banks of Lake Titicaca, they erected one of their temples. Alternatively, the origin of Copacabana might be in the term "Copac Cahuana," or "blue belvedere," from the same language. Following the Spanish Conquest, the ancient Inca temple became a Catholic church dedicated to the Virgin Mary. The natives revered the new deity, deeming her a worker of miracles, and calling her Our Lady of Copacabana. At some point in the seventeenth century – no-one is quite certain when – an image of the Andean saint was brought to Rio by silver merchants. This prompted the building of a small chapel on a rocky point at the southern end of the beach, in a place the local Tamoio Indians called Sacopenapan. It was called "The Little Church of Copacabana," and before long the whole area was known as Copacabana. Urban growth and the degradation of the centre of the city, with its foul and narrow streets, prompted the ruling and trading classes to flee the putrid downtown air. The deplorable living conditions of the majority of *cariocas* – workers and former slaves – resulted in the many epidemics that assailed Rio in those days. 1889 saw the end of the monarchy, and the new republican government instigated reforms intended to rescue the city from the "Middle Ages." Change, however, was slow to happen, and the crisis worsened. The following decade would be scarred by epidemics which took thousands of lives. In 1904, obligatory vaccination was introduced in Rio, producing great indignation among a large portion of the population. Rebels closed the roads with barricades, trying to thwart the efforts of the government's health workers. The government retaliated with brutality, and a virtual state of war was established.

When it was all over, the victorious president Rodrigues Alves announced: "The restoration of Rio's image in the eyes of the world will be the start of a new life." Rio Mayor Pereira Passos embarked on an ambitious reform programme, aimed at improving sanitary conditions in the city centre. Coastal roads were built, and other roads widened, in an attempt to allow the sea breezes to penetrate the fetid city. The city's original lines were being redrawn and open space was the goal, whatever the cost. In the short space of three years, 614 buildings were torn down, the majority of them dilapidated tenements overflowing with people. With no-where to go, legions of homeless took to Rio's many hills, establishing the shantytowns known as *favelas* which punctuate the landscape to this day. The investments in improvements to the city centre were not enough to guarantee its survival as a residential area. Anyone with any money wanted to move away. The social-climbing élite sought a new standard of living, one often modelled on European lines. The desire to emulate the habits of so-called civilized and prosperous nations often resulted in suffering. At the height of summer, gentlemen could be seen in frock coats of English wool, ladies bundled up in long dresses, jackets and shawls. The gentle waving of their delicate fans did little to relieve the heat, aggravated by their outlandish attire. Plenty of perspiration was produced in the pursuit of elegance. The search for the right backdrop to this new lifestyle led to the coast, sculpted by the open sea. The inauguration of the Real Grandeza Tunnel in 1892 was the first step in this direction, linking the still aristocratic neighbourhood of Botafogo to the virtually unreachable Copacabana. The building of the tunnel created dissent among the shareholders of the Companhia Jardim Botânico, the corporation charged with completing the building project in exchange for the tramway concession. Notwithstanding the opinion of the skeptics among their number that "with the exception of one or two decent buildings in Copacabana, the remainder are poor and humble hovels," the Company sponsored a month of festivities after the tunnel's opening, during which the common people were invited to commemorate this new dimension to their city. Advertisements promoting Copacabana claimed "it is kissed by the ocean's fresh breezes, and enjoys a splendid and healthy climate; in truth, it is a sanatorium in this city whose population is sadly decimated by regular and deadly epidemics." Before the advent of the tun-

New thoroughfares were built, such as Avenida Beira-Mar (above, with the Glória church in the background); those who had dwelt in the demolished tenements established shantytowns (top)

The beach with its tiny chapel, dedicated to Our Lady of Copacabana, who gave her name to the neighbourhood, 1908

nel, reaching Copacabana had required firm resolve. There were three ways into the region, each posing its own difficulties. The journey could be made by boat, across the Lagoa Rodrigo de Freitas, then hiking through the hilly pass now known as the Corte do Cantagalo. Copacabana could also be reached via the Ladeira dos Tabajaras, which had been served by regular coaches linking it to Botafogo since 1878. The third option brought one out at the extreme north of the beach at Leme, over tracks that became impassable during the rainy season. The Real Grandeza Tunnel became a focal point for change in the city. Through it would pass the first trams full of holiday-makers and the future residents of Copacabana, making it a district the middle classes were finally able to visit with ease. The vision of paradise offered by Copacabana lifted the spirits of the *cariocas* and gave rise to a growing pride in the exuberant natural beauty which surrounded them. As the steamships bringing European tourists docked in the harbour, 1904's carnival hit summed up widely held feelings by proclaiming Rio to be the "Marvellous City." In 1935, André Filho wrote another carnival song on the same theme, which still stands joyously as the city's official anthem. The discovery of Copacabana's charms led to a collective heightening of awareness among *cariocas* of the beauties of their city. Printed on the tram tickets were reminders of the beneficial effects of Copacabana on

one's health ...
Do your lungs crave salt air?
Flee before the ague gets you.
Rio's sickly centre leave,
Take a tram to Leme!

contemplation ...
Nothing lacks in the
Nature of Copacabana,
Such treats, such riches.
Leave your boring feasts and theatres
For the rocks and the sand
Listen for the ocean on a moonlit night.

fun …
Graceful young ladies, smart young things
Flee the streets, the filthy dust
There's nowhere like Copacabana
For a picnic.

and love …
Hordes of young ones, all in love
Finely dressed dandies with good Havanas
There's no better spot for a flirt
Than Copacabana.

The public relations effort paid off: within a few years, 20 thousand people had moved to Copacabana, among them politicians and members of the government, whose spending power guaranteed development at a feverish rate. Copacabana represented more than simply a solution to old problems; it provided a chance to establish a new way of living. It was the showcase of all that was new and forward-thinking. Between what it promised and what it actually provided, Copacabana became a myth. While other neighbourhoods had to fight for public money, there was always funding for Copacabana; when Avenida Atlântica was once again washed away by heavy seas in 1906, cash for its rebuilding was immediately forthcoming. Life at the seaside set the tempo for the life of the city. On the sand, innovations and fads succeeded one another with the regularity of the breaking waves. The race, creed or status of who or what prompted the innovations was irrelevant. In a society steeped in cultural and social prejudice, those of mixed blood finally found a fertile and receptive arena in which to display their talents. Some of the fads of this era of experiment stuck. For example, in 1902, the English barber Wallace Green happened to invent the beach towel. After giving a customer a shave, Green decided to go for a dip in the ocean, and made for the beach, his barber's towel in hand. Having nothing to sit on, not even a newspaper – which is what most people used – he spread his towel out on the sand and made him-

The Real Grandeza Tunnel changed the life of sleepy Copacabana; within a few years thousands of people were living there. The garden (below) on Avenida Atlântica, now the Praça do Lido, and the Copacabana Palace still under construction, 1922

self comfortable. Soon everyone was stretching out on their own towels. Unwittingly, Green had established a habit which to this day fuels a colourful part of Rio's fashion industry.

The most democratic of all "carioca" habits: bathing in the sea, the 1920's

Europe in the Tropics

In 1919, in the early days of the "Copacabana phenomenon," Epitácio Pessoa (who had been the Brazilian representative at the Treaty of Versailles, which determined the destiny of defeated Germany after World War I) became President of the Republic, imbued with "international values." Elected on a ticket which promised to bring the country into the era of "modernity" that he had seen in France, the President took to extremes the Rio élite's habit of emulating European customs – but not to the point of breaking with old prejudices. In 1921, the same Epitácio, considered progressive, vetoed the presence of black or *mulatto* players on the Brazilian international soccer team. If Pelé had been around then, he would never have played. In spite of such dichotomies, officialdom's intention was to show what was changing in the country, even if the telling of it was more onerous than the change itself. In order to raise the profile of the country he wished to change, Epitácio contracted foreign loans in order to sponsor celebrity visits from across the seas. This series of visits began in September of 1920 with the King and Queen of the Belgians, Albert and Elizabeth, who arrived here after a two-week journey aboard the warship *São Paulo*, which had been especially dispatched to Europe to fetch them. Attended by due ceremony, the couple spent 24 days visiting Rio, Minas Gerais and São

Epitácio Pessoa won the presidency by promising to modernize Brazil, and Copacabana could not be left out. The idea of building a hotel on Rio's most beautiful beach was born

The hotel was intended to host visitors to the International Exhibition of 1922 (above), but was not completed in time. Below, Otávio Guinle's Hotel Palace, hitherto the city's most luxurious

Paulo, and were shown everything that was worthy and exotic in the new nation: they even camped for three days in the Atlantic rainforest in the mountains of Teresópolis, and indulged in leisurely sea bathing on Copacabana beach. The Brazilian Government's hope was that word of everything that pleased Belgian royalty or other guests of similar calibre would be spread throughout Europe by the journalists who accompanied the visitors. Convinced of the effectiveness of this strategy, the President then established an even more ambitious objective: to use the commemoration of the centenary of Brazil's independence as an occasion for making the country known and respected worldwide. The plan was to hold an important exhibition in Rio; friendly nations would show off their wares in a dozen custom-built, palatial pavilions. Despite the considerable expense involved, the likely benefits of the venture seduced the opposition parties and even the more critical sectors of the press. From the authorities' point of view, the Independence Centenary would provide a unique, not-to-be-missed opportunity to thrust Brazil to the forefront of world attention. However, things didn't quite work out that way. Notwithstanding the huge expense of assembling the pavilions for the "friendly nations," and in spite of repeated invitations to their governments, the Presidents of only two nations – Portugal and Argentina – turned up in support of the event. Bereft of the leaders of the great powers, the dream of transforming Brazil into a focus (albeit fleeting) of international attention was not to be. It had never occurred to the leaders of the Brazilian Government that the result of the venture might be frustration and failure. On the contrary, official megalomania saw to it that no effort or expense was spared in the effort to delight the expected Heads of State or to ensure the success of the festivities. The recently discovered marvels of Copacabana could not to be left out of the set designed to dazzle the visitors; a new hotel, in keeping with the high profile of the event, was needed. With this in mind, Epitácio Pessoa went out in search of associates with the means to build a hotel unlike any other in South America, to be noted for its sophistication and the splendor of its location, on the most beautiful beach in the capital of the Republic. The plan called for partners who were experienced, and, above all, daring. After all, once the festivities were over, Copacabana would revert to being a distant and underpopulated neighbourhood. Huge doses

of optimism coupled with an almost blind faith in the future were needed to envisage, in that isolated spot, an enterprise sustained by only occasional guests. Epitácio decided to submit the project to Otávio Guinle, owner of Rio's Hotel Palace and leaseholder of the Hotel Esplanada in São Paulo, the most luxurious establishments in their respective cities. Although the entrepreneur accepted the proposal, he made it a condition that a casino be included in the plans for the new hotel, as a way of rendering it financially viable. The condition was accepted, although ultimately the Government reneged: during the construction of the hotel, legislation was enacted restricting gambling to spas, and soon after the opening of the hotel, gambling was prohibited outright, in 1924, throughout the country. The choice of Otávio Guinle to lead the construction of the first hotel in Copacabana was not an accident. His family was the richest in the country, thanks to the empire founded by his father, Eduardo Palassin Guinle; a *gaúcho*, or native of Rio Grande do Sul, of French origin, in 1886 he had won the bid to build the port of Santos and operate it for a period of 100 years. From this well would spring, for two generations, the wherewithal for hugely successful investment in other fields: the hotel business, the generation and distribution of electricity, tramway companies, real estate, textiles, a bank, insurance, imports and construction. For almost half a century Guinle and his descendants were also the greatest philanthropists and patrons of the arts in Brazil; they supported several charitable institutions and sponsored classical music studies and performances, even overseas. The Guinle patronage was not limited to classical music: in 1922, Os Batutas, sponsored by Otávio's brother Carlos, with Pixinguinha on flute and sax, made their first European tour. Upon his death in 1912, Eduardo Guinle left an estimated 2 billion dollars, in current values. However, it was never shared out equally between all his heirs. In

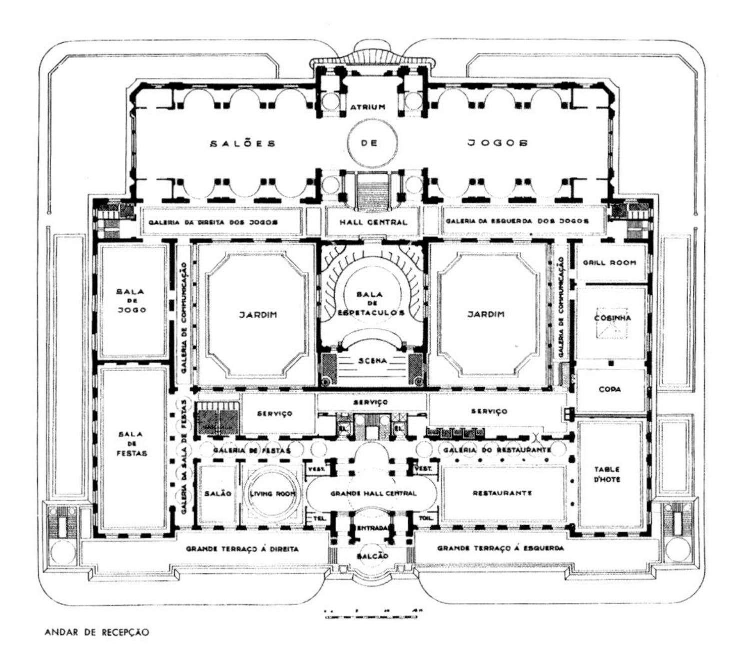

ANDAR DE RECEPÇAO

Successful entrepreneur Otávio Guinle (with the Barão de Saavedra, below, left), who was chosen to lead the hotel project

Redeemable bonds in the Companhia de Hotéis Palace (above) were launched to raise the funding necessary for the construction of the Copacabana Palace (opposite). The design was by French architect Joseph Gire, inspired by the façades of the Negresco and Carlton hotels, on the Côte d'Azur

keeping with the law, his widow Guilhermina kept one half. Of the seven children (five sons and two daughters), Otávio was the only one not to receive his share, as he had been disinherited by his father five years previously. Otávio had married – without his father's permission – a humble American nurse, Monica Borden, who had cared for him during his recovery from typhoid, which he contracted during a trip to the United States. The harshness of this punishment was mitigated by maternal generosity, especially after Otávio Guinle terminated the controversial marriage (with an annulment granted by the Vatican in 1922). Dona Guilhermina invested considerable sums of her own money in her son's hotel project. For Otávio, the hotel became an obsession, and he enthusiastically embraced the mission with which President Pessoa had entrusted him. As a starting point, Otávio purchased an entire city block on Copacabana beach and, in order to obtain the necessary capital, launched redeemable bonds of Companhia de Hotéis Palace on the market. The design of the majestic new hotel was by French architect Joseph Gire, its façade reminiscent of the Negresco and the Carlton hotels, on the Côte d'Azur. Construction work was started without delay, but did not progress rapidly enough to house the Government's guests for the Independence Centenary festivities. Neither the heavy use of imported materials (even the cement was imported from Germany) nor the contracting of foreign workers was enough to avoid delays. Furthermore, the project involved engineering procedures that were very complex for the times; it required foundations almost forty-six feet deep, before pre-fabricated pilings or the machines to drive them existed. To protect the structure of the hotel from raging storms, a massive breakwater had to be built. With so many obstacles to be overcome, the Copacabana Palace would only be completed eleven months after the 1922 commemoration. This initial delay, however, did not blunt Otávio Guinle's enthusiasm. He explained to

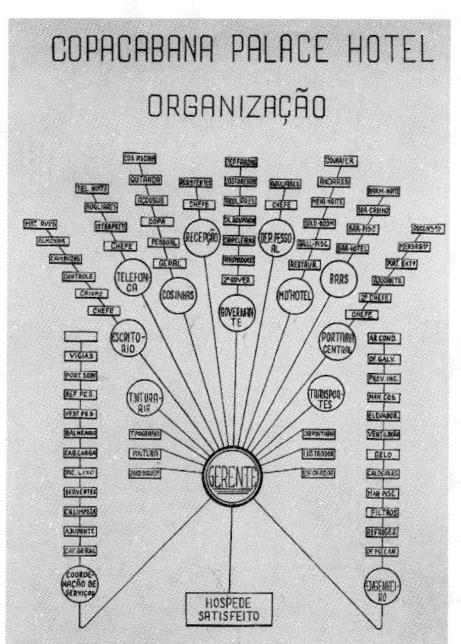

Malta
Phot.

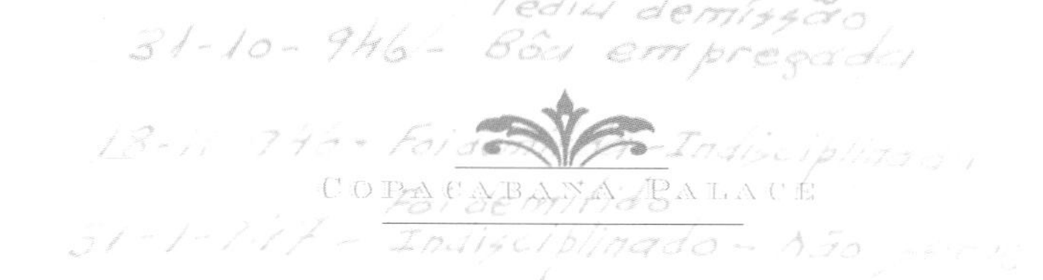

his friends that he was not building a hotel for an event, but a monument of which he would always be proud. For almost half a century, Otávio managed the Copacabana Palace in a very personal, strict and discreet manner. The standards he set reflected an aristocratic temperament, constantly aspiring to good taste and quality, and the vision that the hotel should not be merely a place to stay, but a place for sophisticated leisure and entertainment. Without condescension, Otávio won the loyalty, respect and (in some cases) the veneration of his employees, many of whom stayed with him for decades. In an environment where labour turnover was very low, several of his employees began and ended their professional lives in the hotel. Otávio made his home in "suite B," one of the Copacabana Palace's two presidential suites. Thus he was able to make two daily inspections of all the hotel's facilities, checking such details such as the polish on the banisters or the required shine on the golden buttons of the staff uniforms. It was a common sight to see him running a finger over the furniture looking for traces of dust, or crouching down to inspect under the carpets. Nothing escaped his critical eye. The quality and provenance of the food and beverages served were also strictly monitored, as was the conduct of the barman, instructed to always serve drinks "with grace." Otávio paid huge sums of money to import some of the top professionals of the time from Europe, among them almost the whole team of a gastronomic myth, chef Auguste Escoffier, from the Savoy in London. Noted in his travel diary were the initials GGGSS, a mysterious code which few were able to decipher as *"grand grain, gris, sans sel"* – "large-grained, gray, without salt" – which described the much appreciated caviar served at the Copacabana Palace. A stickler for punctuality, Otávio had installed a device in his suite which allowed him to check on the starting times of the shows playing in the hotel. Any delay resulted in an immediate reprimand. Respect for the public did not, however, extend to concessions for the audience: despite the heat of Rio, the owner of the Copacabana Palace never permitted the entry in his auditoriums of a gentleman without a jacket and tie, and remained, on this matter, obdurate in the face of countless appeals from producers. Staff Policy for the Hotéis Palace Employees was drawn up by Otávio soon after the inauguration of the Copacabana Palace and became a symbol of the times; it remains in effect to this day. Among other things, it pro-

scribes "impertinence in demeanour, attitude, word and gesture; sloth during working hours; indiscretion; curiosity; excessive pandering seeking monetary gain; vanity and negligence in apparel and personal hygiene." The document contains eighteen items which Otávio considered to be essential:

- Behave correctly in the presence of all guests, irrespective of who they are, how much they spend, how long they stay, etc.
- Do not condition to his supposed fortune the service rendered to each guest.
- Show the same attention to the elderly and to the young, and the same patience, without condescension, to children.
- In any and all circumstances, avoid criticism, even if only indirect, of anyone.
- Avoid volunteering opinions. And, when asked, avoid prolonged conversation and chattering with the guest.
- Never contradict a guest, and always attend to his complaints amiably.
- Never, through word or gesture, demonstrate knowledge of the eccentricities of guests, which should go unnoticed.
- Never ridicule the eccentricities of a guest for the benefit of a fellow employee.

Para Otávio Guinle, o hotel não era apenas uma casa de hospedagem, mas um ambiente sofisticado de lazer e diversão. Assim, trouxe da Europa alguns dos melhores profissionais, entre eles, a renomada equipe do "chef" Auguste Escoffier

Little more than one year after the inauguration of the Copacabana Palace, Avenida Atlântica was destroyed by raging seas, 1924 (opposite)

• Never attempt to show efficiency through a hurried demeanour, broadness of gestures, etc. On the contrary, maintain dignity and seek to discharge your duties calmly, never allowing the guest to perceive any upsets. Where there is a problem, it is up to the supervisor to direct the member of staff, as it is his job to keep the guest happy.

• Maintain a certain distance when your presence might be inopportune or indiscreet.

• Never eavesdrop or inquire into the details of a guest's private life.

• Show service to all guests, and, to those departing, avoid exaggerated obsequies and personal demonstrations.

• Regardless of the size of the tip received, consider yourself well remunerated and show your thanks in a respectful manner.

• Avoid the use of jewelry or perfumes and any other items which might indicate frivolity; avoid the consumption of food with an unpleasant odour.

• Maintain yourself and your clothing scrupulously clean, and always be appropriately attired.

• Listen to any reprimand from your superiors with all respect, never contradicting by means of gestures, words or actions.

• Receive orders from your superiors with deference, respecting these orders and obeying them without discussion; demonstrate your enjoyment of your work, respect for your managers and a commitment to your profession.

• Do not smoke during working hours, nor on the hotel premises.

Malta
Phot.

CHAPTER TWO

Mistinguett's Big Night

During the construction of the hotel (below, an advertisement in "Revista Ilustração Brasileira"), Brazil was convulsed by a military revolt. Young officers marched down Copacabana beach determined to depose the Government (above)

The Rich and Powerful at Play

While the Copacabana Palace was being built, Brazil went through some rough patches, underscored by great political tension. It was a time of confrontation between the rural oligarchies of the Old Republic, who had held power since colonial times, and the new urban forces. One of the phases in this battle – and the one with the bloodiest outcome – occurred in July 1922, just a few blocks from the hotel site. During the military uprising which gave rise to the "Eighteen of the Fort" episode, a group of army officers and a sole civilian, bent on deposing the Government, marched along Copacabana beach towards the barricades erected by loyalist troops. At the eleventh hour, other sectors of the military committed to the uprising did not, in fact, support it. Despite the imminence of their defeat, the rebels ripped a Brazilian flag to shreds and gave a piece to each rebel. Of the 29 men to receive the talisman, only eighteen persisted in their revolt; only two survived the subsequent fusillade. The hotel went into operation nine months after this. A searchlight installed on the terrace flashed out greetings in Morse code to all shipping traffic approaching the port of Rio. With few guests (Otávio Guinle raised his champagne glass to toast the six occupied apartments) and deprived of its Casino, outlawed by the Government during the building stage, the Copacabana Palace boasted an auditorium, two restaurants and six salons. Over one thousand employees were at the ready to service the 230 apartments, a ratio which would have been unusual even in the great hotels of Europe. Even so, the daily rate amounted to less than ten dollars, and included all meals and free transportation to the centre of town in the hotel's picturesque coaches. Rooms were generously proportioned and decked out with imported finery: chandeliers from Czechoslovakia, furniture from Sweden, carpets from England; the crystal was Baccarat and the porcelain, Limoges. Seventy-five years on, many of these items remain in their original places and in use, as a reminder of the Copacabana Palace's penchant for tradition. From 1923, practically all noteworthy events, especially those of a controversial nature, either took place in the hotel or were intensely felt in its salons. The inauguration ball provided the first inkling of this. Despite the presence of everybody who mattered in government and in society, it was French dancer Mistinguett who stole the show. The star of Madame Resimi's company, then performing the musical *Ça-gazé* at Rio de Janeiro's Lírico Theatre (with forty chorus girls "who will turn your head"), Mistinguett was hired as the evening's attraction. However, her show was cancelled at the last moment, the star's managers fearing that her appearance would detract from their tour. Somewhat abashed by this situation, Mistinguett made a point of appearing at the ball as a guest; but to widespread frustration, her spectacular legs, which had been insured for 1 million francs, were not exhibited, not even to the photographers who crowded the entrance. The Copacabana Palace offered to return the public their entrance money, but no one took up the offer. The number of guests at the ball exceeded expectations and extra entrance tickets had to be issued; the press gave the event more coverage than when Artur Bernardes, Epitácio Pessoa's successor, stayed at the hotel. "Today, the most grandiose and luxurious example of South American architecture will be launched by Rio high society; news of this will travel the world by way of the tourists passing through." Thus did the *Jornal do Commércio* newspaper of August 14, 1923, herald the first gala night at the Copacabana Palace. "From its terraces lost along the opal sands, and oblivious to the weather and the waves, its guests will gaze upon the unfathomable horizon of the ocean and the natural beauties of our mountain ranges. Within the salons they will contemplate the

Mistinguett, the French star, frustrated guests at the Copacabana Palace inaugural ball by not being allowed to show her famous legs, 1923

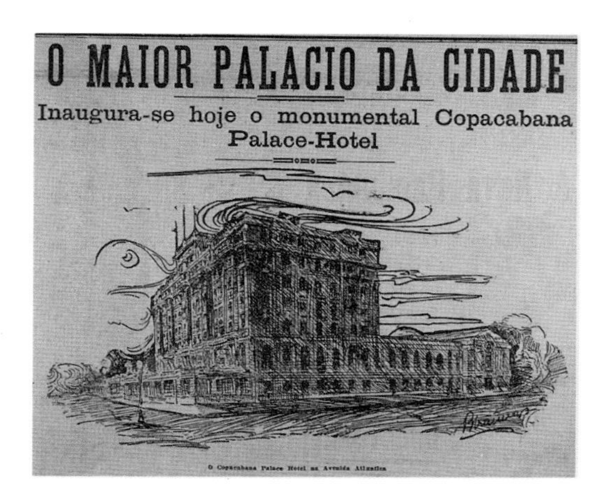

O MAIOR PALACIO DA CIDADE

Inaugura-se hoje o monumental Copacabana Palace-Hotel

manifold colours of the superb, rich ceilings. The southern part of the Copacabana Palace Hotel is taken up by the Casino; with its Carrara marble stairway and Venetian bronze urns it will complete the attractions of the Hotel. Inside, dilettantes will encounter the charming 'boite' of the theatre and the lucullean charm of the grill room with its fine delicacies. Dinner dances, elegant tea parties and other gatherings that our 'grand monde' so appreciate will be held there with charm and the greatest elegance."

From its early years, the hotel recorded the signatures of celebrities from all over the world in its Golden Book. In 1927, Argentine maestro Julio De Caro composed the tango "Copacabana," the first international hit to mention the new neighbourhood by name (opposite)

From Einstein to the Prince of Wales

From the outset, the Copacabana Palace became the city's nerve centre owing to a succession of visits from heads of governments, kings and queens, statesmen, cinema stars, famous musicians and sportsmen. Despite going missing between 1946 and 1965, the Copacabana Palace Golden Book is a veritable treasure, which has registered countless manifestations of satisfaction since the 1920's. The hotel was also the venue of choice for the entertainment of illustrious visitors, as can be seen by the luncheon hosted by press magnate Assis Chateaubriand in honour of Albert Einstein in 1925. The German scientist, by then world-renowned, was the focus of widespread curiosity, attracting crowds (mainly of laymen) to his lectures on the theory of relativity. Einstein repaid the compliments showered on him by the Brazilians with impassioned praise for Rio, which he dubbed "a work of art." He recalled his first sight of the city as being "... one of the greatest emotions of my life." Of the Botanical Gardens he said that "the flora surpasses the fantasies of the One Thousand and One Nights – everything lives and grows before your very eyes." Outpourings of love for the city abounded. In 1927, after a season at the Copacabana Palace, the Argentine violinist and conductor Julio De Caro composed the first international hit to mention Copacabana by name. "From the balcony of

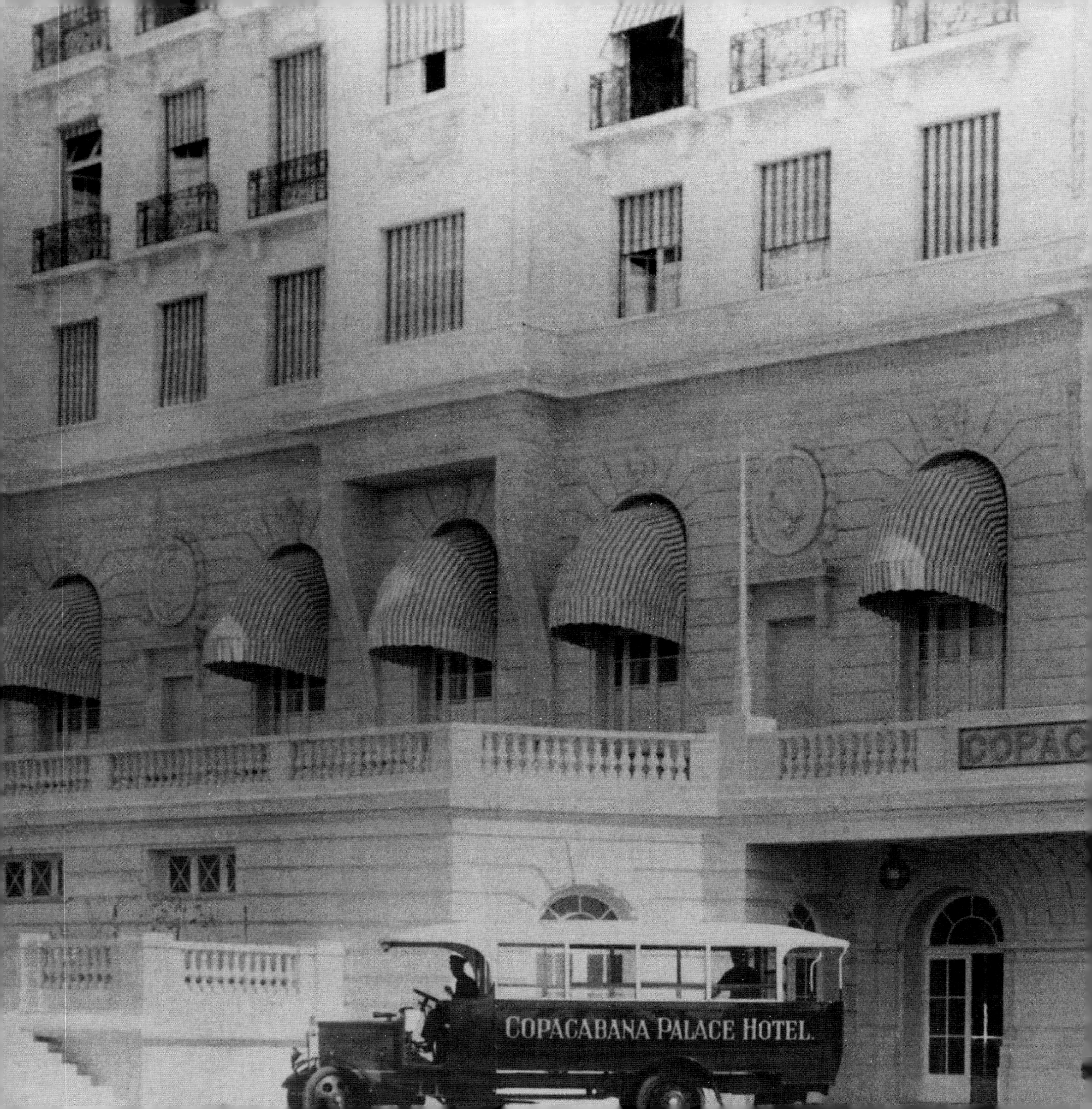
COPACABANA PALACE HOTEL.
COPAC

Transportation to the centre of town in the hotel's picturesque coaches was one of the amenities offered to guests

The arrival of Santos Dumont in Rio de Janeiro in 1928 was marked by tragedy – the seaplane leading the reception committee exploded after falling in the sea, killing all its occupants

my room in the hotel I looked upon the ocean and admired the coastline sprinkled with multicoloured lights," De Caro wrote in his memoirs, fondly recalling his moment of inspiration. "The wind was balmy, the surroundings Dionysiac. It was three o'clock in the morning, and something guided my hand to my music book. I wrote on the page: 'Copacabana' and the subtitle 'Love Nest'. It came out all at once." But not all celebrities' experiences at the Copacabana Palace were as happy as De Caro's. At the end of 1928, early aviator Alberto Santos Dumont, who was 56 and had been living in France since the age of 18, agreed to return to Brazil, in an attempt to cure a depressive condition which had already caused him to be been interned in a Swiss sanatorium. His depression was brought on by a diagnosis of multiple sclerosis and aggravated by feelings of guilt – he agonized over the uses to which aviation was being put. He sent petitions (which went unanswered) to the Society of Nations and gave countless lectures calling for a global ban on all military airplanes. He became so upset at news reports of air crashes and accidents that his friends and employees kept from him newspapers or magazines carrying reports of any such incidents. Santos Dumont was a long-standing friend of the Guinle family, and called on them frequently at the Hotel Raphael whenever they were in Paris. His stay at the Copacabana Palace was due to start on December 3. A group of airmen and intellectuals who were planning to submit his candidacy to the Brazilian Academy of Letters decided to herald Santos Dumont's arrival in Brazil by flying a seaplane over his approaching ship and dropping a message of welcome by parachute. From the deck of the liner *Cap Ancona*, Santos Dumont watched, in horror, as the event turned to tragedy: the seaplane (which bore his name) fell into the sea and exploded. All the occupants were killed. The drama affected the inventor profoundly; he personally participated in the recovery of the bodies, went to all the funerals and then locked himself in his room at the Copacabana Palace for almost a month. Three years later, watching the airplanes involved in the 1932 Revolution fly past, and hearing, in the distance, the sounds of bombing, the Father of Aviation hanged himself in the bathroom of a summer home in Guarujá. The press, gagged, attributed his death to heart problems, and a three-day truce was called between the loyalist and rebel troops. The truce, however, was broken before the three days were up. Unlike Santos

Dumont's sad sojourn in Rio, some incidents which took place at the Copacabana Palace did not make it into the history books. One such episode occurred in 1929 and involved President Washington Luís. The President was shot and wounded by his mistress, whom he used to meet in secret at the hotel. The scandal would have been enough to shake the Government, which had the support of the Church and other conservative groups, but nothing was leaked. Washington Luís was taken to a public hospital, and it was announced that he was undergoing an emergency appendectomy. In 1930, in a less dramatic manner, the President was deposed; a coup annulled the fraudulent presidential elections which had taken place a few months previously. This marked the start of the fifteen years of the first Vargas government. While the political classes were building up a head of steam, social life in the capital of the Republic became even more effervescent. During that busy year of 1930, Rio hosted the first Miss Brazil competition as well as the first Miss Universe competition to be held in Brazil. The candidates crossed the city in open cars to then parade before the jury on the terrace of the Copacabana Palace, watched by the impassioned, cat-calling gallery which crowded Avenida Atlântica. The crown and sceptre of the world's beauty queen went to Yolanda Pereira, of Rio Grande do Sul, amid much celebrating in the streets. For four decades thereafter, beauty pageants were popular in Brazil, and the stuff of dreams for many a middle-class miss. Much swooning and sighing by young ladies ushered in Princes Edward and George in March 1931. Sons of the King of England, at that time they were aged 36 and 35, respectively. (Edward, Prince of Wales, was to succeed to the throne in 1936, but soon abdicated to marry Wallis Simpson, a divorced American. His brother was to succeed him, and reigned as George VI until 1952.) The arrival of the two Princes attracted a large crowd of oglers to the doors of the Copacabana Palace and merited a day off for schools and public offices. They arrived on the SS *Alcântara* wearing tropical pith helmets and impeccable white uniforms. President Getúlio Vargas and his entire cabinet awaited them, decked out in tails and top hats. While officially a holiday, the trip was also intended to ease negotiations regarding the repayment of 253 million pounds, owed by the Brazilian Government to the British Rothschilds. The itinerary included a tour of the south of the country and a visit to the Paraná Plantations, a

EINSTEIN NO RIO

Albert Einstein on the Copa terrace during a luncheon offered by Assis Chateaubriand

large British-owned farm in the Londrina region. But this last stage of the trip could not be completed due to the heavy rains flooding the region. During their retreat to the nearest city, on the border of São Paulo, their cars became bogged down in the mud, and the royal party completed the ten final muddy miles on foot. The sacrifice was worth it, however. Due to this mishap, part of the agenda was cancelled, and the visitors were able to spend more time in Rio de Janeiro. The two Princes soon let it be known that formal engagements were not the only ones they had in mind. Witnesses relate that the royal brothers were not averse to the odd drink, and sometimes became majestically inebriated. Thus, during a reception that Carlos Guinle hosted at his mansion on Botafogo beach, the Prince of Wales set aside all semblance of sobriety or protocol and surprised his fellow guests by trying to catch, with his hands, the fish swimming in the fountain. It was during this same party that Edward met Negra Bernardez, whom he admitted to being in love with for many years. The mother of two sons, popular in *carioca* society, Negra was attractive and divorced. Although she spoke English, she enchanted the prince by talking to him in Spanish, and helped to rescue him from the empty conversation of the avid young ladies that followed him everywhere. (An example of this implacable siege was an album full of photographs, with which he and his brother were presented upon their departure, of all the unmarried daughters of Rio's illustrious families displaying their prettiest smiles.) That first meeting between Edward and Negra was followed by others; they often bathed in the sea in front of the Copacabana Palace. Edward did not think twice about taking off his beach robe and presenting it to Negra's son, young Lauro, who had admired the coat of arms embroidered on the garment's pocket. Other attempts to charm his potential ladyfriend were not so straightforward. The Prince even proposed a private flight – just the two of them – in the airplane carried on one of his escorting ships. Members of the royal party discreetly sought out Negra and suggested she decline the invitation: the airplane was missing some parts and it was feared that Edward would, in his excitement, decide to fly it anyway. The Prince of Wales's return to England after eighteen days in Brazil brought an end to the romance begun in Carlos Guinle's home. Negra Bernardez preferred it that way. She refused to respond to the pleas of her suitor (reiterated in copious future corre-

spondence) that she take up residence in London. She based her decision on her firmly held desire to keep and educate her two sons in Brazil, even though she was Uruguayan by birth. The youngest son, Manuel Bernardez Müller, was to become our first renowned social columnist, under the pen name Jacinto de Thormes. 1931 brought yet another illustrious guest to the Copacabana Palace: Frank Lloyd Wright, famed as the greatest architect in the United States. He virtually walked off the jury during the 1st International Exhibition of Tropical Architecture in order to support a Brazilian students' strike. The strike was prompted by the dismissal of architect Lúcio Costa from his management position at the School of Fine Arts, an establishment entirely controlled by conservatives. The Copacabana Palace became the strike headquarters, where Wright made speeches in defense of the pioneer of Brazilian modern architecture. Lúcio Costa lost his job anyway, but Wright was rewarded for his support of the movement – just as he was departing, the student strikers serenaded him in front of the hotel. Throughout the first Vargas government, from 1930 to 1945, practically all of the country's cultural output came from Rio. Inevitably, Copacabana became cultural headquarters. The feverish excitement of its nights gathered momentum, and it seemed that Copacabana had no time for sleep. After three years in office, Getúlio Vargas revoked the law which had kept the casinos closed since 1924. This new legislation directly benefited the Copacabana Palace, ready and waiting with the largest and most luxurious gaming rooms in the city.

Dinner in one of the sophisticated salons of the Copa was an obligatory event for politicians, heads of state and stars visiting the Marvellous City

Guests observed the "Graf Zeppelin" from the hotel windows during its first flight to the Southern Hemisphere in 1930

Peace in times of war

Innovative in so many ways, the architectural design of the Copacabana Palace started a tradition of façades turned towards an element which had hitherto been treated with astonishing indifference by *carioca* builders: the sea. Until the Copa established the trend, and the rest of Avenida Atlântica followed suit, few of Rio's mansions or large homes faced the ocean. The Copacabana Palace not only lent luxury and prestige to the seaside but also sent seaside property prices soaring. During the Second World War those who had opted for life at the seaside had reason to question their decision. As of 1942, when German submarines began sinking Brazilian merchant ships, Copacabana, for a while at least, monitored the situation more closely than the other neighbourhoods of Rio. When war against the Axis was declared in August of that year, the population was apprehensive of possible attack from the Atlantic. Fear increased in proportion to the national involvement in the conflict; it was further fuelled by the installation of an American air base in Natal, the nearest continental point in the Americas to the fighting in North Africa. To protect the city from possible naval bombardment, the authorities ordered "severe preventive measures" along the seashore. All residents and traders adjacent to the beaches were ordered to turn their lights out or put up blackout curtains. The lamp-posts on Avenida Atlântica were even painted black, and in the Praça do Lido, three blocks from the Copacabana Palace, metal objects donated

by the population formed a "war pyramid" of material for the future manufacture of weapons. Hitler's navy never did appear, and it was soon perceived that Copacabana ran no risk, or if it did, no-one was too concerned about it. Nightlife in the area virtually ignored the effects of the blackout. On the beaches, passionate couples got carried away in the darkness and frequently ended up being arrested for indecency. In the hotel's Casino, gambling and entertainment grew unchecked, the crowds swollen with the presence of American officers in transit. In July 1944, while the population listened on their radios to the news of a distant war and musical hits such as *Aquarela do Brasil*, some five thousand Brazilian soldiers (out of a contingent which would exceed 25 thousand) were shipped off to the Italian front. Four hundred and fifty-four soldiers would die and over two thousand would be wounded, but one year later the troops returned in triumph: Rio threw the biggest party in its history. The élite commemorated the victory with two days of dancing at the Copacabana Palace and at

the Country Club, that other citadel of Brazilian high society. The dizzying growth of Copacabana never stopped, not even for the war. It grew upwards, the only way it could accommodate the legion of new residents. This trend began in the 1930's, when the Empresa de Construções Civis, a construction company which owned most of the available plots, prioritized the sale of plots to developers of residential buildings. Skyscrapers, emblematic of the much-desired modernity, replaced the stately mansions of the beginning of the century. In the early days, Copacabana's vertical growth – now at saturation levels – was hailed with enthusiasm. In 1935, an editorial in the magazine *Beira-Mar* (a type of official bulletin covering Rio's South Zone) extolled the new buildings, pointing out that they were a boon to local trade and stating that they increased values of neighbouring property, promoted social interaction and "attracted civilization." The penthouse apartments at the tops of these buildings were truly upper-crust living. The very rich inhabited them, and from their windows one could more comfortably contemplate historical events: the first voyage of the *Graf Zeppelin* to the Southern Hemisphere or the inauguration of the Statue of Christ, both occurring in 1931. The following year, the samba

schools organized their first collective parade, giving rise to what is today Rio's greatest cultural attraction. Day after day, the city quite naturally – without the subterfuge employed by Epitácio Pessoa – put itself on the international map and won its place in the heart of the world. Rio was fashionable, and Copacabana was the height of fashion in Rio.

Foi imponente a inauguração da Piscina do Copacabana Palace

Inaugurou-se a piscina do Copacabana Palace

For those guests who did not enjoy the beach, the Copa offered the luxury of one of the city's most beautiful swimming pools, opened in 1935, and the services of a swimming instructress, Ruth Behrensdort (below, between two pupils)

Staff records in the hotel archives tell some of the history of the Golden Room stars. Norma Bengell, Tatiana Leskova (also at right) and Vitória Bonaiuti, who became famous as Marlene (below)

COMPANHIA HOTEIS PALACE
RIO DE JANEIRO
Registro de Empregado n.º 2943
DEPARTAMENTO DE DIVERSÕES
NOME NORMA BENGELL
FILIAÇÃO Pai Christian F. Bengell
Mãi Maria da G.G. Bengell
CARTEIRAS Profissional N.º 3376 Série 102 Identidade N.º
Reservista N.º Categoria Reserva de
Sindicato Matrícula Saúde
Registro Fiscalisação de Hoteis N.º Estrangeiro N.º
Contribuinte do Instituto dos Comerciarios N.º
Estado Civil solteira Instrução secundaria Idade 22 anos. Data nascimento 21/2/932
Nacionalidade brasileira Lugar do nascimento D. Federal
Residência Av. Copacabana 152 apt. 46 Data da admissão 18/9/54
Quando Estrangeiro Data em que chegou? É naturalisado? Equiparado?
É casado com Brasileira? Tem filhos Brasileiros?
Categoria e Ocupação habitual artista Salário Cr$233,30 - diarios - Cr$7.000,00 mensais
Para trabalhar das às horas com o intervalo de horas para refeição e descanço:
e aos sábados das às horas num total de horas semanais.
BENEFICIÁRIOS Pai -
Mãi -
Assinatura do Empregado Norma Bengell
Data
Data da saída 15 de Janeiro de 19[illegible]

COMPANHIA HOTEIS PALACE
RIO DE JANEIRO
2ª VIA Registro de Empregado n.º 2198
DEPARTAMENTO DE DIVERSÕES
NOME TATIANA HELENE LESKOFF
FILIAÇÃO Pai George Leskoff
Mãi Helene Madem
CARTEIRAS Profissional N.º 73565 Série 73 Identidade N.º
Reservista N.º Categoria Reserva de
Sindicato Matrícula Saúde
Registro Fiscalisação de Hoteis N.º Estrangeiro N.º 175818
Contribuinte do Instituto I. A. P. C. N.º 1.542.909
Estado Civil solteira Instrução sim Idade 25 anos. Data nascimento 6/12/922
Nacionalidade Francesa Lugar do nascimento França
Residência Rua Tavares de Macedo n. 12 Data da admissão 1/11/948.
Quando Estrangeiro Data em que chegou? É naturalisado? Equiparado?
É casado com Brasileira? Tem filhos Brasileiros?
Categoria e Ocupação habitual bailarina Salário Cr$[illegible] - diarios
Para trabalhar das às horas com o intervalo de horas para refeição e descanço:
e aos sábados das às horas num total de horas semanais.
BENEFICIÁRIOS
Assinatura do Empregado Tatiana Helene Leskoff
Data da saída 17 de agosto de 1949.

COMPANHIA HOTEIS PALACE
RIO DE JANEIRO
2ª VIA Registro de Empregado n.º 1955
DEPARTAMENTO DE DIVERSÕES
NOME VITORIA BONAIUTI
FILIAÇÃO Pai Vitorio Bonaiuti
Mãi Antonietta Bonaiuti
CARTEIRAS Profissional N.º 27.302 Série 62a. Identidade N.º
Reservista N.º Categoria Reserva de
Sindicato Matrícula Saúde
Registro Fiscalisação de Hoteis N.º Estrangeiro N.º
Contribuinte do Instituto I.A.P.C. N.º 1.112.319
Estado Civil solteira Instrução sim Idade 26 anos. Data nascimento 22 de Janeiro de 1922
Nacionalidade brasileira Lugar do nascimento São Paulo - Est. de São Paulo
Residência Av. S. Sebastião 199 apto. 201
Quando Estrangeiro Data em que chegou? É naturalisado? Equiparado?
É casado com Brasileira? Tem filhos Brasileiros?
Data da admissão 1 de Março de 1948
Categoria e Ocupação habitual cantora Salário Cr$266,00 diarios
Para trabalhar das às horas com o intervalo de horas para refeição e descanço:
e aos sábados das às horas num total de horas semanais.
BENEFICIÁRIOS
Assinatura do Empregado [illegible]
Data
Data da saída 17 de Agosto de 1949.

The Setting for the Stars

In 1938, during a decade of all-embracing prosperity and growing diversification of its attractions, the hotel opened the Golden Room, Copacabana's first great show venue. For many years great names in show business from Europe, the United States and South America would perform there. For the opening night, the house was packed with four hundred guests in formal attire. Each had paid the equivalent of thirty dollars (a fortune at that time) for the privilege of dining and hearing *chansonnier* Maurice Chevalier. Over subsequent decades the Golden Room was to host many other famous artists, such as Yves Montand, Lena Horne, Dionne Warwick, Josephine Baker, Ella Fitzgerald, Gilbert Bécaud, Marlene Dietrich, Lucho Gatica, Amália Rodrigues, Edith Piaf, Nat King Cole, Sammy Davis Jr., Jean Sablon, Charles Aznavour, Sarita Montiel, Tony Bennett, Ray Charles, Sacha Distel, Yma Sumac, Johnny Mathis and countless Brazilian performers as well. As of 1944, with the arrival of Austrian producer Baron Max von Stuckart, the Golden Room created a concept of musical theatre which delighted audiences for many years with the sophistication of its sets, the lavish wardrobes, the originality of its scripts and the faultless beauty of its chorus girls. This concept was inaugurated with a show entitled *Em busca da beleza* [In Search of Beauty], which boasted "the most beautiful Brazilian girls," selected by Von Stuckart himself. Among them was Maria Della Costa. Hailed later for her qualities as a dramatic actress, Maria was responsible for the climax of the show, during which she appeared with her breasts covered only by diaphanous fabric – an extremely daring act for those days in Brazil. Another performer in the same musical was the young ballerina Tatiana Leskova. A Frenchwoman born to Russian parents, she had decided to abandon the company with whom she had been touring South America and remain in Rio. Her training in classical dancing guaranteed her a lengthy career in the Municipal Theatre, as prima ballerina for fourteen years and later as director of the ballet corps. By 1946, José Caribé da Rocha had taken over the artistic direction of the Copacabana Palace; he produced a musical called *O circo* [The Circus], enhanced by solos from flautist Benedicto Lacerda and the arrangements of maestro Radamés Gnatalli, who had migrated from classical music to popular. Soon after, Caribé put on *Vitória-régia* and broke with tradition by intermingling artists of different social classes, not usual practice on Brazilian stages. The show featured singers Sílvio Caldas and Carmen Costa; also in the cast were high society's youthful Elisinha Coelho and the Copacabana Girls, snowy white ballerinas recruited from the foremost ballet schools in the city. *Fantasia & fantasias* [Fantasy & Fantasies] was the focus of polemic from the start. In 1955, defying the law forbidding the participation of anyone under the age of 21 in evening performances, Caribé da Rocha dared to include in his cast some lovely but under-aged models. The big star was to be Norma Bengell, only 17. Notwithstanding her parents' consent (officialized by a Notary Public) and a license from the authorities, her proposed appearance resulted in a lengthy lawsuit, which was reported on daily by the press. Debates, editorials, outpourings of support and others of distaste only fuelled the public's expectations. Once *Fantasia & fantasias* (by now nicknamed "The Emancipated Girls") was finally allowed to be performed in the Golden Room, it played to a full house every night. Once again, Copacabana was breaking with tradition. After

The Golden Room hosted the stars, among them "chansonnier" Yves Montand (above) and dancer Paul Drapper (below)

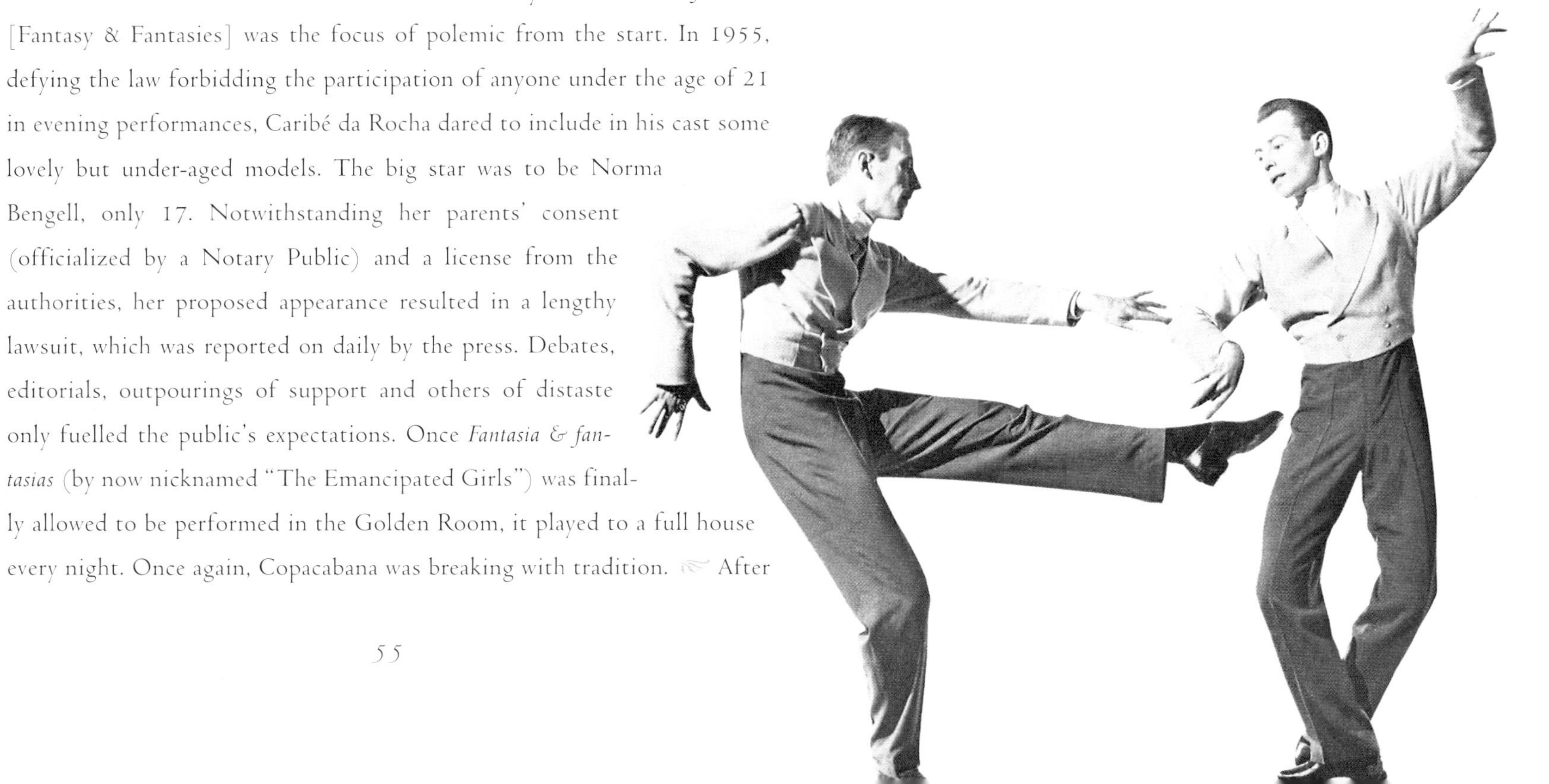

Henriette Morineau (right)

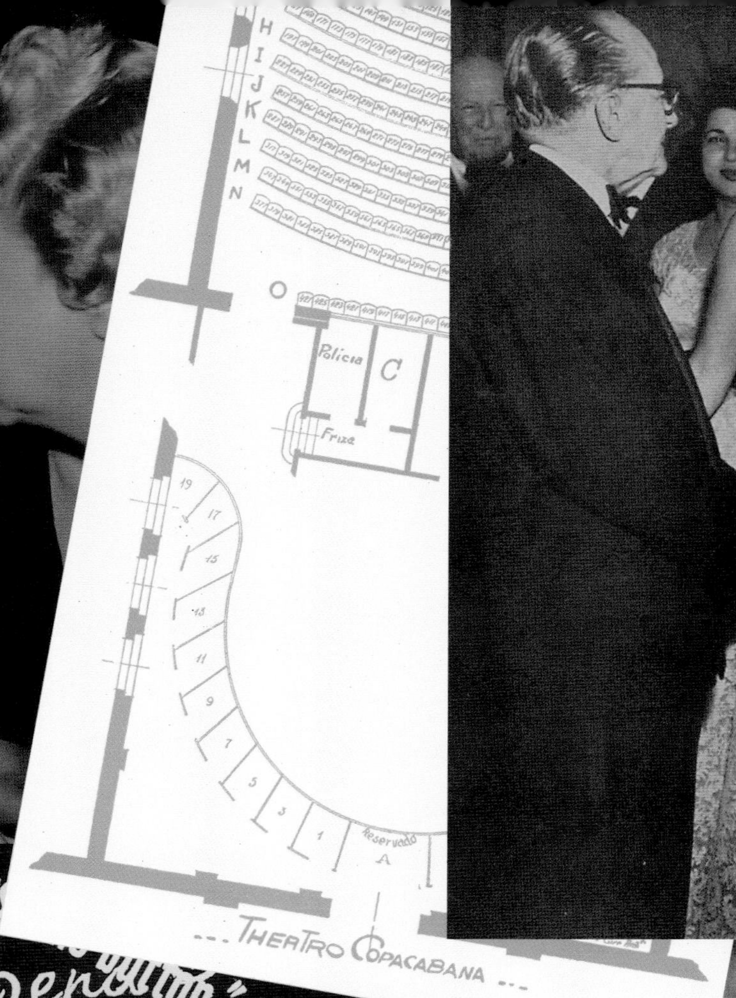

Susan Hayward

Maria Della Costa

Dorival Caymmi

Lena Horne

Amália Rodrigues

Carlos Machado
Oscar Ornstein

Sammy Davis Jr.
Murilo Neri

ogue
RESERVADA
AV. PRINCESA ISABEL, 23 PHONE 27-0100
night and day
HOTEL SERRADOR 1 St. FLOOR PHONE 42-7119

Marlene Dietrich

"Rio de 400 janeiros"

Marlene Dietrich on stage (above), in her dressing room at the Golden Room (below, right) and on the cover of "Cinearte" magazine (opposite). On opening night, four hundred guests applauded Maurice Chevalier (below)

the *Fantasia & fantasias* season, a behind-the-scenes incident took place which was to show that not all prejudices were so easily overcome. In 1956, Otávio Guinle vetoed the proposal of director Silveira Sampaio to use white chorus girls in the role of race-horses and coloured girls as their jockeys. The owner of the Copacabana Palace demanded an inversion of the roles, and Silveira Sampaio, a hugely successful professional in his field, resigned. "I, and only I, choose the colours of my horses," he said, defying the racial prejudices of Otávio Guinle. The show was never performed. The celebrities appearing at the Golden Room helped to turn the Copacabana Palace into an international source of gossip. Something peculiar seemed to affect the artists – possibly something to do with the exotic, passionate ambiance they found themselves in. This often led to strange happenings, to the delight of the ever watchful press and fans. Although the stories vary with every telling, these behind-the-scenes incidents are part of the soul of the Copacabana Palace. One of the most picturesque is told by Fery Wünsch, *maître d'* for over forty years. One night in 1959 the crowded Golden Room eagerly awaited Marlene Dietrich's first show of the season. Shortly before curtain time, the Blue Angel urgently summoned Wünsch to her dressing room: "Fery, I want a champagne bucket full of sand." While an employee was quickly despatched to the beach for the sand, Marlene explained, "Just look at this dress ... clinging to me ... I can't even get down the twenty steps to the ladies' room for a miserable pee ..." But that was not the sum total of Marlene's eccentricities. Her dressing room had to be entirely refurbished because, on the eve of her opening night, she had decided that the shade of pink paint on the walls was not exactly that specified in the contract. The artist also insisted that the champagne she consumed so liberally, lettuce, chicken and mineral water all be flown out to her from Paris, by Air France. Luxury left its mark on the history of the Golden Room. In 1961, impresario Abraão Medina put on *Skindô*, the most expensive show the country had ever seen. With a technical team imported from the United States and radio and television stars, the

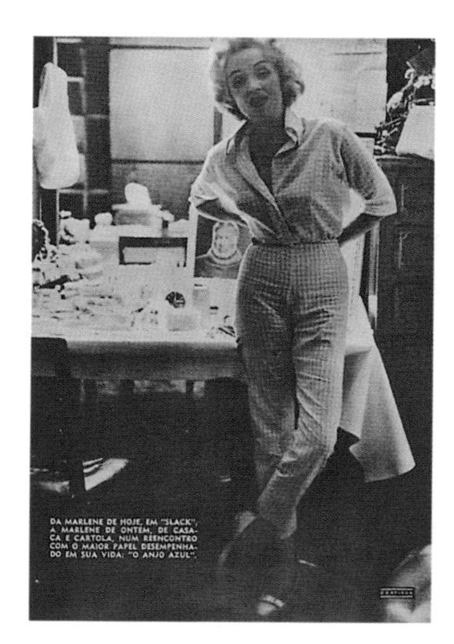
DA MARLENE DE HOJE, EM "SLACK", A MARLENE DE ONTEM, DE CASACA E CARTOLA, NUM REENCONTRO COM O MAIOR PAPEL DESEMPENHADO EM SUA VIDA: "O ANJO AZUL".

Marlene Dietrich
ANNO XI N. 437
RIO DE JANEIRO, 15 DE ABRIL DE 1936
Preço para todo o Brasil 2$000
J. Luiz

RIO MAGAZINE

The Copacabana Palace's annual Sweepstakes Week consisted of seven days of balls and festivities which coincided with the Grande Prêmio Brasil, the principal Brazilian horse-racing event

"Rio de 400 janeiros," a show by Carlos Machado (above), Nat King Cole on the Copa terrace (below) and Maria Della Costa (above, right, in the middle with outstretched arms) in the show "Em busca da beleza"

musical was a great success in Rio, but flopped in Europe. The tour was marred by a certain lack of foresight on Medina's part. There was simply no public in Paris in the middle of the summer holidays; the company even had trouble finding places to eat. Despite the failures abroad, musical revues continued to enjoy good audiences in Rio. As of 1962, there were shows such as *O teu cabelo não nega* [Your Hair Gives you Away], produced by Carlos Machado and based on the work of Lamartine Babo, who died on the eve of the first performance; *Tio Samba* [Uncle Samba], by Americans Sonia Shaw and Bill Hitchcock; and *Frenesi*, by Carlos Manga. Between one show and the next, the Golden Room hosted lightning seasons featuring great international attractions, not all of which were blessed with success. Disaster struck mega-star Tony Bennett, contracted for a three-night stint in 1963; he found himself looking at an audience of exactly sixteen people, seated at two tables. The host of one of the tables was his Brazilian impresario. The star of *I Left my Heart in San Francisco* took the situation in hand and, under a solitary spotlight, loosened his bow-tie, seated himself on one of the stage steps and sang through the entire programme; it was an unforgettable experience for the lucky few present. In 1965, the Golden Room, managed once again by Carlos Machado, put on *Rio de 400 janeiros* [Rio of 400 Januaries]. Inspired by the four-hundredth anniversary of the founding of the city, the revue was judged by the critics as the most luxurious ever. The production required three months of rehearsals and involved 150 professionals, between technicians and performers; *Manchete* magazine stated that

the show had "the most admired collection of *mulattas* in Rio." The wardrobe consisted of five hundred luxurious costumes, designed by Gisela, Carlos Machado's wife, who made a name for herself as one of the greatest designers on the Brazilian stage. Premieres such as these were true happenings in the city's life. Opening nights at the Copacabana Palace were timed to coincide with the Grande Prêmio Brasil, the principal Brazilian horse-racing event, which carried huge social weight and attracted visitors from all over the country. The Copa put on a Sweepstakes Week, with banquets, balls, parties and prize-giving ceremonies. High society turned out en masse, as did foreign guests and anybody who was anybody. At the end of the 1960's, Haroldo Costa put on productions such as *Rio Zé Pereira, Sua excelência, o samba* and *Aquarela musical,* this last the final long-running show staged in the Golden Room. 1970 saw the closure, for the first time after the disastrous fire of 1953, of the Golden Room; sadly, audiences for such luxurious and sophisticated musical revues had disappeared. From then on, the traditional Copacabana Palace showhouse opened only sporadically. In 1972, on one of these rare occasions, Dionne Warwick altered the content of her standard international show to include songs by Chico Buarque de Holanda, always so carefully policed by the censors of the military regime of the time. Warwick, exhilarated by the public's enthusiastic response, abandoned her routine and danced along with the audience. Over 25 years later, the memories of this happy encounter influenced her decision to buy a house in Rio, where to this day she spends part of her time. The Golden Room re-opened in the 1980's, leased by Ricardo Amaral. It was becoming increasingly difficult to accommodate foreign stars in a venue designed for smaller audiences, so Amaral settled on a more eclectic programme which favoured Brazilian artists, among them comedians Chico

"Skindô" was a great hit in the Golden Room, with Betty Faria (above, on stage, and in her dressing room with dancers Letícia Neri and Marta Botelho)

Anysio and Jô Soares. On the night of the re-inauguration, the clock was turned back with a show by Cauby Peixoto (a star of the golden days of Brazilian radio) requiring formal wear. But any harking back to the past came to an end the following day, when the audience appeared wearing jeans and open-necked shirts. Any doubts that an era was over were dispelled in 1981 when a competition to select pin-ups for girlie magazines was held on the Golden Room's stage. The country then made the acquaintance of *gaúcha* Maria da Graça Meneghel, or Xuxa, who won the title of "Panther of the Year." Her glorious nudity stamped all over *Status* magazine, Xuxa was on her way to stardom and riches. One of the rare foreigners to perform in the Golden Room during this time was Sammy Davis Jr., who returned to Rio in 1982, after fourteen years, for his second season at the Copacabana Palace. Davis took the opportunity of getting together with coloured musicians and actors in the home of singer Eliana Pittman, daughter of the late saxophonist Booker Pittman. This was a message for his critics back in the United States, who objected to his seeming lack of interest in the fight for racial equality. "I have always supported coloured causes such as those of Malcolm X and Luther King," he explained. "I just cannot condone the Black Panthers' violence."

Zsa Zsa Gabor with ambassador Hugo Gouthier and producer Baron Max von Stuckart (far left), who created the concept of the musical revue in the Golden Room with its elaborate sets, luxurious wardrobes and gorgeous chorus girls

Carnival on Fire

During the 1950's, Brazilian films were at the height of their popularity, surpassing even Hollywood hits in their audience figures. Crowds flocked to watch dozens of national films, mainly humorous musicals. The critics dismissed these productions as vulgar and tasteless; "*chanchadas*," they were disparagingly called. But the "*chanchadas*" were hugely successful, and gave many a producer, director and actor their foot in the door of the market. The Copacabana Palace served as the exclusive backdrop for one of the classics of that time: the comedy *Carnaval no fogo* [Carnival on Fire], in which the musical numbers were supposed to be part of a Golden Room show. The cast included the duo Oscarito and Grande Otelo, sweethearts Anselmo Duarte and Eliana Macedo, and the eternal villain José Lewgoy. In addition to breaking all box-office records, the film provided six of the "in" tunes for the 1950 carnival.

The hit movie "Carnaval no fogo," with Oscarito, Grande Otelo, Anselmo Duarte and Eliana Macedo, was set at the Copacabana Palace

COPACABANA
CASINO
RIO DE JANEIRO

Chapter Three

Gentlemen, Place your Bets

Black, Seventeen

From its very first days the Copacabana Palace was the antechamber to Brazil, hosting its most illustrious visitors and serving as a backdrop for almost all events of any importance that occurred in the country over four decades. But the hotel also suffered some serious setbacks. In April 1946, Marshal Dutra, who had been elected President at the end of the previous year, outlawed gambling and closed down all the casinos in the country. It was widely believed, but not necessarily true, that this measure reflected the wishes of the President's ardently Catholic wife, Carmela. While it was certainly true that "Dona Santinha," as she was known to her friends, had campaigned hard in this matter, the closure of the casinos should more accurately be attributed to widespread pressure from conservative sectors, especially the all-powerful Church. During the presidential elections, brigadier Eduardo Gomes, the candidate beaten by Dutra, had promised to "banish gambling from the country." The larger, more influential newspapers took up the cry, reporting with such partiality that a suicide would only get a mention in print if he were a gambling man, drowning in debt. This fanaticism spread to the Government. The text of the decree signed by Dutra was more like a manifesto than an administrative act. Gambling had been on the scene since the 19th century, but the decree stated – without any foundation in fact – that "the moral, judicial and religious traditions of the Brazilian people are contrary to games of chance." The

COPACABANA
CASINO-THEATRO
Rio de Janeiro
-o-
FICHAS
Nas Mesas. Lácres.......... 600...Na Ca
" " . Amarellas......... 450..."
" " . Brancas.......... 550..."
1.600
-o-
FICHAS DE
Nas Mesas. Cinzas......... 1.000...Na
" " . Azues......... 1.000..."
" " . Verdes......... 1.050..."
" " . Verdes Claras.... 1.000
" . Rosas......... 950
5.000
CASINO COPACABANA
RIO DE JANEIRO
CRUZEIROS
CLUB MAR DEL PLATA
PESOS
3167
100
1000
REIS
20

Fun, elegance and glamour in the gaming rooms of the Copacabana Palace Casino

closure of the casinos (which numbered 79 throughout the country) represented not just the end of a golden era in Rio, but unemployment for almost 40 thousand people, including artists and technicians involved in the entertainment industry, the natural business partner of gambling. By and large, the press paid no heed to the chorus of protest from the unemployed, choosing not to share with its readers the plight of the newly out-of-work. All the papers seemed interested in publishing were endless stories of the immoralities of the Vargas dictatorship, so recently terminated. Between 1939 and 1945, while Europe and then the United States were embroiled in the Second World War, Rio nightlife was truly outstanding. At the gaming tables of the

Copacabana Palace, fun, elegance and glamour were oblivious to the horrors of war. Most of the time. Of course, there were plenty of losers, for whenever luck is unceasingly challenged, it tends to run out sooner. Between the magical shows at the Golden Room and the allure of the roulette wheels, there was no pause for rest and life seemed to run on passion and dreams. Gambling tales are populated by those who lost millions, and by those who won millions without risking a penny of their own. Among the latter was a smooth-talking Portuguese with gentle manners who rose to fame during the 1940's. Posing as the heir to the Marquis of Pombal, he obtained the unwitting sponsorship of several gullible Portuguese businessmen for his gambling activities. Lacking the charm of the bogus Marquis, but protected by the powerful in the Republic, another compulsive gambler, Benjamim Vargas – Getúlio's brother – spread panic among staff and patrons of the Copacabana Palace Casino with his habit of trying to chase away bad luck with bullets. One famous night, down on his luck, "Bejo" laid his revolver upon the green baize and announced his bet for all to hear, "Black, seventeen!" It was not a good hunch. When the roulette ball settled cheekily and unafraid in number nine, an apprehensive silence settled upon the table. Of an easily combustible nature, always above the law, Bejo was already reaching for his gun when the croupier drew first, announcing the providential result, "Black, seventeen!" The President's brother collected his winnings, put away his gun and gambled no more that night. The Copacabana Casino was leased to third parties, as Otávio Guinle never wanted to run it himself. In the lease contract, the Copacabana Palace insisted on clauses that obliged the tenants to maintain a permanent cast of two orchestras, a male or female singer "of national renown," twelve chorus girls and four crooners; Nelson Gonçalves, Ciro Monteiro, Carmen Costa and Carmélia Alves were, at one time or another, among these. (Even after the closure of the casinos, the Golden Room continued to elevate to stardom singers such as Doris Monteiro, Ivon Cury, Marlene, Jorge Goulart and Nora Ney, who were immensely popular due to their live radio shows on Rádio Nacional and Rádio Tupi.) Rio society, which until the late 1930's partied only in private, began to dance in the Casino ballroom to the sound of imported bands, such as Simon

A permanent cast of two orchestras, a singer, twelve chorus girls and four crooners, among them Carmélia Alves (below), was maintained

Boutman's band, which played its fox-trots there for twelve years. An added attraction at the Casino were the foreign chorus girls. Brought in every year for a stint of never more than three months, they had first to get through the strict selection process of the producers. Firing up the male audience, the girls shared the limelight with the guest stars and at times even obscured them. Young, lovely and liberal, they provoked incendiary passions in an era when virginity was a hurdle overcome only by marriage. Off stage, the presence of these girls lent gaiety and charm to the private parties hosted by society bachelors – and many a romance started at these social gatherings ended up in marriage.

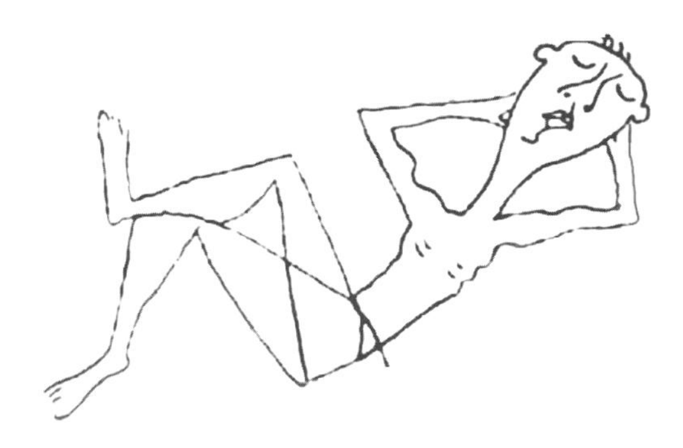

The School for Scoundrels

The Copa swimming pool was the headquarters of the Clube dos Cafajestes, a group of well-born young men who were the perpetrators of most of the outrageous pranks recorded in Rio between the 1940's and 1960's

Despite not being terribly interested in gambling, a group of well-born young men made the nightly rounds of the more luxurious casinos of Rio, using charm and cash to win the company of the beauties on the stage. To further their amorous ambitions, the band of seducers – among them Nelson Baptista, Antenor Mayrink Veiga, Horácio Carvalho and Armando Serzedello Corrêa – organized a weekend on the paradisic isle of Brocoió, which Otávio Guinle had lent to his nephew Jorginho. (The island is in Guanabara Bay and was bought by Otávio Guinle in the 30's. He built a mansion there, as a gift for his second wife, "Baby," the Argentine-born Maria Beatriz Campbell.) During the party, they put paid to the hotelier's unrivalled wine cellar, complete with its generous collection of rare wines and his private stock, the largest in Brazil, of Château Pétrus and Château d'Yquem. It is fair to say that this brotherhood of conquerors was the forerunner of the Clube dos Cafajestes [Scoundrel's Club], another group of equally well-born young men who left their mark on Rio. From the 1940's to the 1960's, headquartered at the Copacabana Palace swimming pool, the Cafajestes were the perpetrators of practically all the outrageous pranks recorded in the everyday chronicles of Rio life. On many an occasion they took on the role of daring and unpunishable challengers of current morality. In 1949 they organized a march to protest a decision by the chief of police forbidding

the presence in Copacabana of bathers dressed "merely" in swimwear, without a blouse or shirt. On a sunny Sunday, the beaches teeming with people, they paraded in open cars down Avenida Atlântica wearing top hats and tails; beside them were prostitutes hired for the occasion, clad in "daring" two-piece bathing suits under elegant fur coats. The protesters chorused a rowdy can-can, poking fun at the authorities and proclaiming their preparedness to give their bodies for the cause of sartorial liberty. Hosts of memorable parties, the Cafajestes proclaimed allegiance to one law only: "respect the wife of your friend." This led them into confrontations with husbands, fiancés and intendeds who were not a part of their coterie; some of these fights turned into pitched battles. But none of these skirmishes, in which they usually came out on top, took place at the Copacabana Palace. Nor did they involve the police, who shied away from their illustrious surnames or their military status, as in the case of their founder and leader, Carlos Eduardo de Oliveira, "Commander Edu," an officer in the Air Force. Muscle and clout were not always critical to the success of the Cafajestes' undertakings. In 1953, some of them were ceremoniously summoned to a three-night bash in the Copacabana Palace's Presidential suite. The cause of the celebration was the separation of Dominican playboy Porfirio Rubirosa; after forty days of marriage to millionaire Barbara Hutton, he had

Otávio and Beatriz Guinle with Benita Campbell (below) on the paradisic island of Brocoió, where Jorginho Guinle and his friends annihilated Otávio's collection of rare wines, 1935

won himself a divorce and a million-dollar settlement. As luck would have it, this bacchanalian celebration coincided with the austere Otávio Guinle's trip to Europe, which permitted Rubirosa's guests license never before known on the hotel's premises. Although it consisted mainly of "young men of good breeding," the democratic philosophy of the Clube dos Cafajestes allowed them to harbour members of other social strata. The most notorious of these "hangers-on" was Ibrahim Ahmed Sued, the son of Lebanese immigrants, who in the late 1940's was starting his career in journalism as a photographer's assistant. Astute, determined and conscientious, Ibrahim worked his way to success; for over forty years he produced the most influential social column of the Brazilian press. News items in his column often produced ripples through society, and he became an institution and a household name; his bizarre catchwords were absorbed into everyday language. The Copacabana Palace was the seat of Ibrahim's dominions; more often than not, he could be seen at his private poolside table, where the mighty would call to share precious nuggets of information for the daily column.

A notorious member of the Club, Ibrahim Sued dances with Barbara Rush in the Golden Room in 1955 (above) and poses with the 1957 debutantes (left)

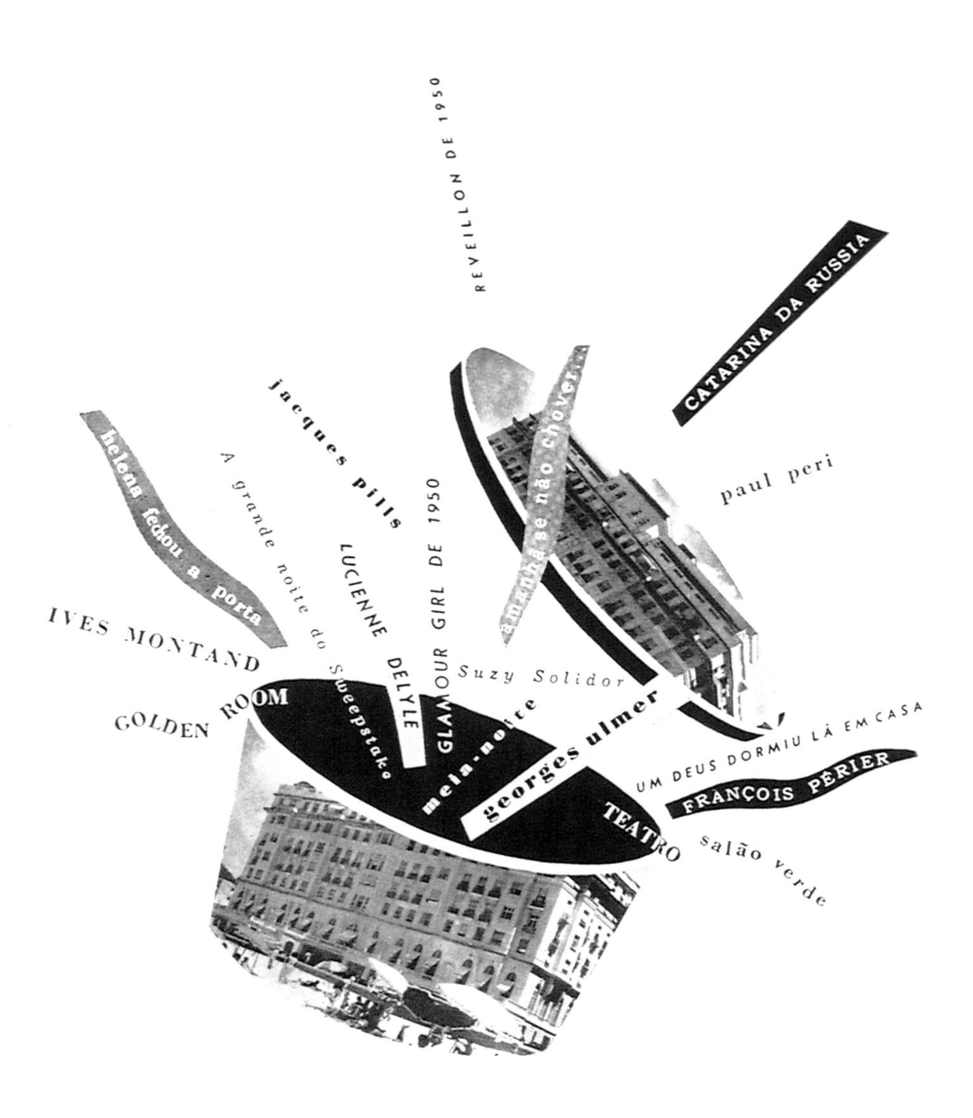

Oscar Ornstein (opposite), the hotel's public relations man as of 1946; he dreamed of becoming the "Brazilian Ziegfeld"

Mr. Copacabana

With his Casino outlawed, Otávio Guinle sought other ways to keep his hotel in the limelight; to this end he stepped up the production of artistic events and professionalized the Copacabana Palace's relationship with the press. In 1946 he hired Oscar Ornstein, a German who had worked at Urca and Quitandinha casinos. For 24 years Oscar was much more than a public relations man; he helped turn the Copacabana Palace into a permanent locus of events. His first task was to organize Mexican singer Pedro Vargas's tour. Oscar not only managed to attract a large audience, but also introduced two important innovations; the shows were sponsored and broadcasting rights were sold to radio stations. A Hamburg Jew who later lived in Vienna, Oscar spoke several languages and had worked as a photographer with the Keystone agency. His arrival in Rio had been traumatic. Fleeing from the Nazis, he arrived in May 1941 with one hundred dollars, a suitcase and a camera. These were confiscated from him weeks later by the management of the Hotel Novo Mundo, on Flamengo beach, to guarantee settlement of his hotel bill, which Oscar could no longer pay. With nowhere to go and no more than the clothes on his back, he took to sleeping on a bench in Praça do Lido. On his third night "camping out," Oscar was spotted by Von Stuckart, who lived in a neighbouring building. He spoke to Oscar in German, felt sorry for him and gave him a job as an audience photographer at the Urca Casino. From then on,

COPACABANA

Ornstein revolutionized "carioca" nightlife by importing international attractions, Abbey Lincoln (below), and encouraging Brazilian artists such as Moacyr e Cia. (above)

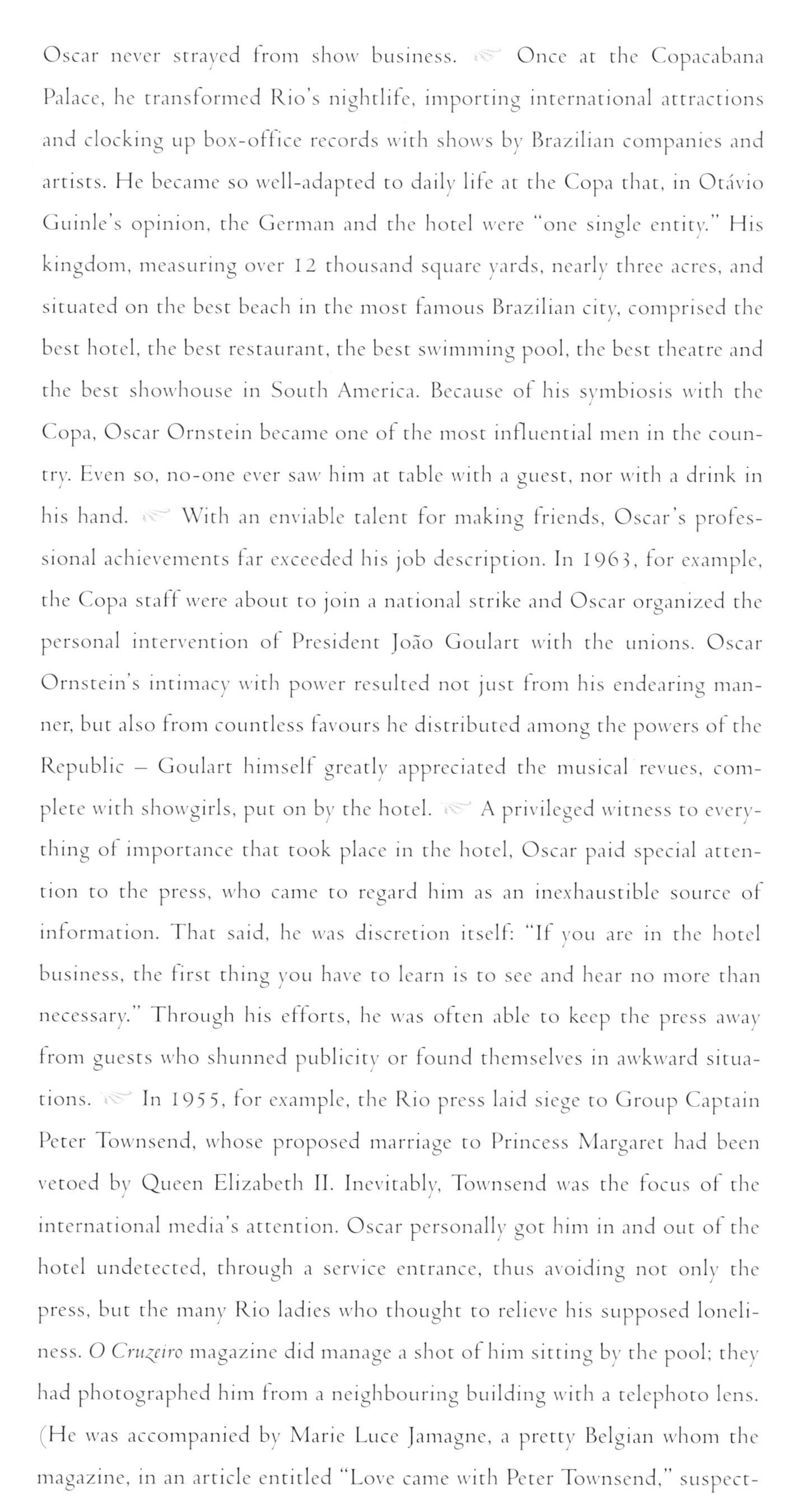

Oscar never strayed from show business. Once at the Copacabana Palace, he transformed Rio's nightlife, importing international attractions and clocking up box-office records with shows by Brazilian companies and artists. He became so well-adapted to daily life at the Copa that, in Otávio Guinle's opinion, the German and the hotel were "one single entity." His kingdom, measuring over 12 thousand square yards, nearly three acres, and situated on the best beach in the most famous Brazilian city, comprised the best hotel, the best restaurant, the best swimming pool, the best theatre and the best showhouse in South America. Because of his symbiosis with the Copa, Oscar Ornstein became one of the most influential men in the country. Even so, no-one ever saw him at table with a guest, nor with a drink in his hand. With an enviable talent for making friends, Oscar's professional achievements far exceeded his job description. In 1963, for example, the Copa staff were about to join a national strike and Oscar organized the personal intervention of President João Goulart with the unions. Oscar Ornstein's intimacy with power resulted not just from his endearing manner, but also from countless favours he distributed among the powers of the Republic – Goulart himself greatly appreciated the musical revues, complete with showgirls, put on by the hotel. A privileged witness to everything of importance that took place in the hotel, Oscar paid special attention to the press, who came to regard him as an inexhaustible source of information. That said, he was discretion itself: "If you are in the hotel business, the first thing you have to learn is to see and hear no more than necessary." Through his efforts, he was often able to keep the press away from guests who shunned publicity or found themselves in awkward situations. In 1955, for example, the Rio press laid siege to Group Captain Peter Townsend, whose proposed marriage to Princess Margaret had been vetoed by Queen Elizabeth II. Inevitably, Townsend was the focus of the international media's attention. Oscar personally got him in and out of the hotel undetected, through a service entrance, thus avoiding not only the press, but the many Rio ladies who thought to relieve his supposed loneliness. *O Cruzeiro* magazine did manage a shot of him sitting by the pool; they had photographed him from a neighbouring building with a telephoto lens. (He was accompanied by Marie Luce Jamagne, a pretty Belgian whom the magazine, in an article entitled "Love came with Peter Townsend," suspect-

ed was more than the Group Captain's private secretary.) Another to enjoy the protection of Oscar Ornstein was Edward Kennedy. It happened in the wee hours of a night in 1961, when President Kennedy's younger brother attempted to take three women he had just met in the Bolero, one of the most notorious nightspots in Copacabana, up to his suite. The night manager consulted Otávio Guinle, who, "for security reasons," scuppered the plan. The episode was soon brought to the attention of the American consul in Rio, who saw no diplomatic reason for interfering in the case; Oscar then successfully took it upon himself to ensure the story did not reach the press. Alongside his duties at the hotel, Oscar developed a busy career as a producer, going so far as to lease the theatre from the Copa. This involvement with the artistic world rooted him even more firmly in the city and earned him the nickname in the United States of "Mr. Copacabana," thanks to Earl Wilson, the *New York Post*'s influential columnist. Oscar confessed to his friends that his dream was to become the "Brazilian Ziegfeld," but not all the shows in which he invested were successful. While he did enjoy a few commercial successes, he was better known for the grandeur of his productions and the generosity of the fees paid to the performers than for the financial results of his shows.

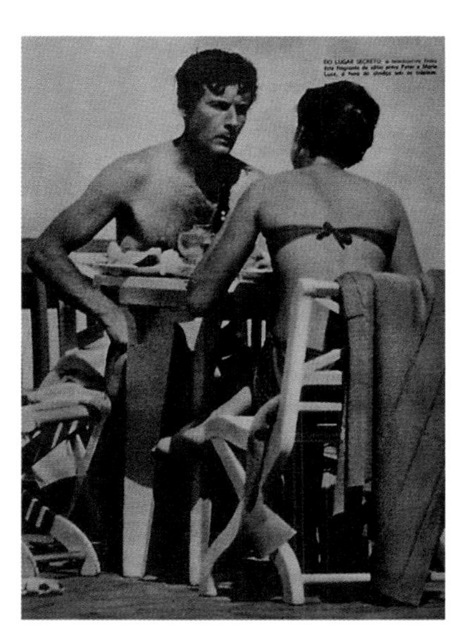

Oscar Ornstein protected Peter Townsend (left) from the siege set up by the international media and also brought talents such as Georgia Brown (left); his wife Margarette (above) is seen here in a rare photograph taken by Ornstein himself

· Theatre and Casino Foyer ·

Drawing Room

· Luncheon Room ·

Salon

Copacabana Palace
APARTAMENTOS
Livro de Ouro
Copacabana Palace
LIVRO DE OURO
Nº 1

Chapter Four

All the World's a Screen

The American movie industry made the official acquaintance of Copacabana with the film "Flying Down to Rio," starring Dolores Del Rio (opposite)

Rio in Malibu

In 1933, the American movie industry discovered Copacabana with *Flying Down to Rio*. Starring Dolores Del Rio, the film marked the debut of Fred Astaire and Ginger Rogers, who, albeit in supporting roles, appeared in a musical number called "The *Carioca*." Production costs for the film were high, and shooting took place almost exclusively at a mock Copacabana Palace built at the RKO studios in Hollywood. The movie's most famous scene relies on trick photography to depict lovely chorus girls dancing on the wings of an airplane flying over a fake Copacabana. The beach in the background was actually Malibu, where all the outdoor scenes were shot. Geography notwithstanding, *Flying Down to Rio* succeeded in situating a story in a joyous, festive, sun-drenched city. Visits by the rich and famous to Rio multiplied, especially after Europe became embroiled in the Second World War. In an increasingly dangerous world, Brazil offered a liberating mix of gambling, heat and fun. During this period the Copacabana Palace's Golden Book registered, among many others, the signatures of Tyrone Power (1938), Henry Fonda (1939), Errol Flynn (1940), Bing Crosby and Douglas Fairbanks Jr. (1941) and Walt Disney (1942).

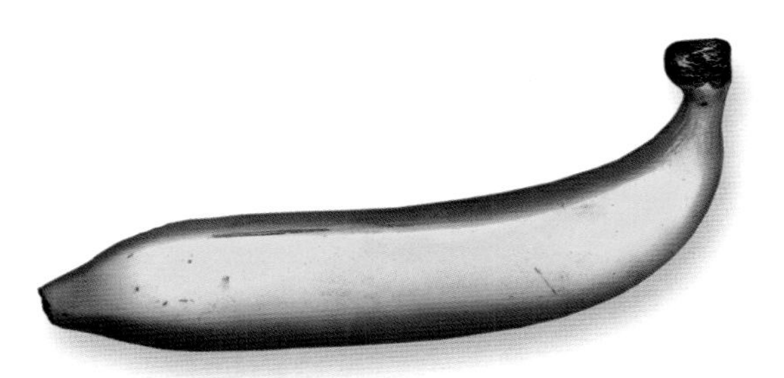

Carmen without baubles

Although plenty of film directors had already chosen Rio as their next fount of inspiration, a star who would epitomize the union of Hollywood with the tropics was still lacking. In 1939, American impresario Lee Schubert watched a show starring Carmen Miranda and the Bando da Lua at the Urca Casino. Schubert was impressed, and when he invited the group to appear on Broadway in a musical revue called *Streets of Paris*, Carmen and her companions accepted. Although the number at the Urca Casino had amounted to no more than six minutes, it was enough to open the doors to the great studios. In 1940, before signing her first contract with Fox, Carmen returned to Rio to perform a charity show at the same Casino in Urca. The artist's reception by the high-society *carioca* audience was chilly, the applause sparse. Horrified, Carmen left the stage in tears, convinced that the Brazilians thought her too "Americanized" and no longer admired her talent. The episode was to traumatize her for the rest of her life. Having completed six films in Brazil, Carmen went on to act in fourteen more in the United States. She became the most famous Brazilian performer in the world, a caricature of the exotic and musical world the Hollywood directors of the day so wanted to reproduce on film. She wore colourful turbans decked with tropical fruit, enormous hoops in her ears and every imaginable species of glittery bauble. Barely five feet tall, she teetered on six-inch platform shoes. The success of the so-called

Brazilian Bombshell was truly resounding. Thanks to her, songs such as *Mamãe, eu quero* and *Tico-tico no fubá* became international hits. In 1946, Carmen paid the highest income tax of any woman in the United States. And, of course, her producers also profited from Carmen's success. The film *The Gang's All Here*, for example, had the highest box-office earnings for 1943. (In it, the artist performs her best-known number, singing *The Lady in the Tutti-frutti Hat.*) In 1954, marital problems and an interminable succession of films, shows and travels led Carmen to a nervous breakdown. A return to Brazil, after an absence of fourteen years, was indicated as the best therapy. However, Carmen feared the antipathy that she imagined the Brazilians felt for her. But Aurora Miranda went to Los Angeles and, after much insisting, managed to bring her sister back to Rio. On December 3, a very depressed Carmen and her family moved into the Copacabana Palace for what would turn into a four-month stay. Moved by the sight of the tropical garland that decorated her suite, Carmen murmured, "At last, Brazilian flowers ..." Doctor Aloysio Salles was called to examine Carmen Miranda and found her profoundly depressed and in a seriously debilitated state of health. Upon leaving, the doctor affixed a warning, which was to remain there for a good long time, to the door of Carmen's room: "No visitors, no exceptions." For thirty days Carmen did not feel well enough to leave her room. Once, she attempted a walk on the beach, but no sooner had her feet touched the sidewalk than she gave up the idea. On another occasion she startled her family when, standing at the window of her room, she erupted into noisy laughter, something she had not done for months. She then explained to her astonished sisters that she had just seen a guest lose his bathing shorts as he dived into the pool. Carmen recovered slowly, aided by the loving care of her family, the oatmeal porridge that her mother prepared for her every day, and, later on, the doctor's permission to receive visits from close friends. Her social life, however, did not extend beyond the limits of the Copacabana Palace. She watched *Fantasia & fantasias* in the Golden Room, accompanied by visiting American actress Elaine Stewart. Gradually Carmen returned to her former happy self, and returned to the United States on April 4, 1955. Before leaving, she invited Dr. Salles to share a glass of champagne with her. For the first time in those four months, room service at the Copa conveyed an alcoholic beverage to

Carmen Miranda's suite. In August, Carmen died of a heart attack in Los Angeles. She was buried in Rio, and her funeral brought into the streets crowds comparable only to those accompanying the coffin of Getúlio Vargas the year before. It was an outpouring of love – whose existence she had doubted for so many troubled years – for the Brazilian Bombshell. In 1995, all the objects from Carmen's room at the Copacabana Palace were donated by the hotel to a museum founded in Rio to honour the actress.

Carmen Miranda took refuge in the Copa for four months, recovering from severe depression. Opposite, scenes from the musical "The Gang's All Here," one of the singer's greatest successes

Myths and Mysteries of the Annexe

The construction of an eleven-storey Annexe solved the space problem at the hotel

In July 1943, Copacabana celebrated its fiftieth birthday. Two years later the Second World War came to an end, and a few months after that the Vargas dictatorship fell. It was a time of hope and euphoria. In the United States, immense financial and technical resources, which had previously been devoted to the war effort, were now being channelled into civilian use. Hollywood had never been so glamorous, and the American way of life supplanted the European as the model to be followed by the rest of the world. The signs of these new times reached Brazil via Copacabana, rendering the neighbourhood ever more welcoming and eclectic. Its 110 city blocks and 2.5 square miles could not help but provide a breeding ground for the new customs. Copacabana was a laboratory where novelties and foreign attitudes mingled with local ingredients, helping to concoct the "*carioca* way." It was a style that did not meet with everyone's approval. The São Paulo newspapers, for example, regularly criticized the new society springing up in Copacabana, accusing it of corrupting an imagined "Brazilian model." However, what was happening in Copacabana was not a classic case of de-nationalization. Copacabana rejected mere mimicry of imported standards (whether European or American) by blending multiple influences to create the unique "Copacabana way of life." In this the neighbourhood could well have been a pioneer even in international terms. A

BEBA
Coca-C
BEM GELA

The all-suite Annexe was the height of modernity. Opposite, a cover by Michel Burton for "Rio Magazine"

master's thesis prepared in 1991 by social scientist Simone Andrade Pereira maintained that, while it was inspired by big American cities just after the Second World War, Copacabana in the 1950's invented a new, playful use of urban space. According to the same thesis, Copacabana thereby became one of the most vibrant places of the era, forging a distinct personality and a previously unheard-of sociability. At the height of these transformations, the Copacabana Palace was the vibrating nerve centre of the neighbourhood. Increasingly sought after, the hotel was frequently obliged to turn guests away for lack of accommodation. Otávio Guinle then decided to expand, building an eleven-storey extension on the land occupied by the tennis courts. The work was begun in 1946, and two years later the Annexe was inaugurated. Its chief characteristic was that all accommodation units featured a living room separate from the bedroom. To the frustration of those who resisted change, the design of the new building did not follow the neo-classical architecture of the hotel. On the contrary, its lines were in the contemporary style. This opting for what was new, rather than aesthetic or functional, was motivated by the desire to be up-to-date, something bubbling post-war Copacabana demanded. Likewise, this desire for modernity became a characteristic of those who chose to stay in the Annexe – or live there, as several politicians and businessmen did during subsequent decades. A separate lobby and reception and a great predominance of Brazilians among its guests gave the Annexe its own, less formal atmosphere, which was very distinct from that of the Copacabana Palace. License and freedom which the old Copa, faithful to the precepts of tradition, would never allow, were fully enjoyed: one could receive guests in one's rooms. Many a mysterious encounter was enacted in the Annexe, which soon became the source of inexhaustible folklore of illicit trysts, inadmissible adventures and illustrious betrayals. Stories abounded, and there is little point in seeking accurate versions. One told of a secret passage that traversed kitchens, storerooms, indoor patios and dimly lit corridors, connecting Renault's hairdressing salon to the rooms in the Annexe, thereby facilitating the transit of ladies who did not wish to be seen. Infidelity in high society or romances between powerful big-spending gentlemen and ambitious girls generated gossip which was often the main theme of conversations and whispers in the salons of Rio society, then the capital of the

RIO MAGAZINE

LUIZ BANDEIRA
CANTANDO NO "MEIA-NOITE" DO COPACABANA PALACE
Copacabana
MARCA REGISTRADA
INDÚSTRIA BRASILEIRA
LONG PLAY 33⅓ R.P.M.
JANTAR DANÇANTE
QUARTETO EXCELSIOR
CLP 3012-A
1. APROVEITA A MARÉ (W. Silva - H. de Carvalho)
2. O ORVALHO VEM CAINDO (Noel Rosa - Kid Pepe)
3. BAIÃO GRACIOSO (Zaccarias)
4. IMPLORAR (Germano Augusto - Kid Pepe - Gaspar)
(MLP-053)
FABRICADO POR SOM INDÚSTRIA E COMÉRCIO S.A.
Av. NELSON CARDOSO, 627 - ESCRITÓRIO: AV. RIO BRANCO, 25 15º AND RIO DE JANEIRO
DIREITOS RESERVADOS DE EXECUÇÃO PUBLICA E RÁDIO TRANSMISSÃO
E SEU CONJUNTO
ABRE A JANELA
ISTAMBUL
YAYA
LISBÔA ANTIGA
ARRASTA A SANDALIA
SOMETHING S GOTTA GIVE
MAMBO BRASILEIRO

The Annexe was the setting for secret trysts, illicit loves and dangerous adventures, providing a constant source of gossip for the city's elegant salons and social columns

Republic. The press did not usually relate this gossip, even when enriched with details of high drama. In two different stories, the protagonist dies of a heart attack *in flagrante delicto*. In the first, friends of the deceased (a highly placed member of São Paulo Governor Adhemar de Barros's team, who was supposed to be in an official meeting at the time) got him out of the Annexe – and out of the headlines – by frog-marching him through the lobby as if he were drunk. In the other story, faced with the naked corpse of an important banker, the socialite with whom the deceased had maintained an affair did not hesitate to phone the man's wife and politely ask for instructions.

Copacabana was the most welcoming and metropolitan of neighbourhoods and the hotel was its nerve centre

THE TRADUCERS' TRIANGLE

A superficial view might lead one to the conclusion that the history of the Copacabana Palace was chiefly one of parties and dissipation. Not so. For a time, between the 1940's and the founding of Brasília, the Copa and the Catete Palace (seat of government in the old capital) shared the distinction of being the great incubators of national political plots. In those days, the Bife de Ouro [Golden Steak] restaurant, its bar and the Annexe formed a triangle within which state secrets, party maneuvers and other conspiracies were the order of the day, or rather, of the dawn. And, avid for news that often circulated there before it reached Congress, the press was always in attendance. The good food, impeccable service and refined decoration of the restaurant mattered less than the discretion of the waiters and the aura of privacy. It was a place where all the world converged, but especially the traducers. Across the tables of the Bife de Ouro (thus named by Assis Chateaubriand, in reference to the prices on the menu), bankers, businessmen and politicians caroused the nights away, crafting in the smoke from their cigars the figures for their shady deals and the destiny of the country. In 1955, for example, one of these many finagles helped to depose President Carlos Luz and block the *coup d'état* designed to prevent Juscelino Kubitschek, the elected successor, from taking power. Congressman Vítor Issler was living at that time in suite 53 of

The Bife de Ouro was famous not only for its good food and impeccable service but also for the discretion of its waiters and its aura of privacy

Juscelino Kubitschek and wife with Oscar Ornstein in the Copa, the stage for a ploy to ensure the president took office

the Annexe, and it was there, on the night of November 10, that two colonels and a group of congressmen connected to Kubitschek drew up a motion for impeachment which would, the following morning, overthrow Luz from the Presidency of the Republic; he was charged with being "in a dubious and unknown place." His whereabouts, however, were general knowledge. With the support of the Navy, he and several allies had boarded the cruiser *Tamandaré* and were sailing to Santos to gather forces and stage a reprisal. The plan was frustrated when the ship became the target of "shots of warning and intimidation" from Copacabana Fort, under the orders of the War Minister, Marshal Teixeira Lott, whom Luz had tried to dismiss the day before. From the verandah of the Copacabana Palace, crowded with curious guests, the waiters who had served coffee and drinks to the participants of the meeting in Issler's apartment watched, with ears plugged, as the 305-millimeter shells were fired from the Fort. Political drama did not always affect the Bife de Ouro community in a uniform manner. In August 1961, Jorginho Guinle's arrival from Los Angeles coincided with the unexpected resignation of President Jânio Quadros. Jorginho, proudly exhibiting a list of American stars he had invited for the following year's carnival in Rio, cruised around the restaurant trying to find reporters, a politician, anyone who would listen to his plans. Apprised of the gravity of the situation, the playboy railed against the lack of interest in his stories from the United States: "OK, the President has quit ... But what's that got to do with carnival?" Jorginho was absolutely right, and the carnival of 1962 was just as thrilling as previous ones. João Goulart, the vice president, took over the Government until the *coup d'état* of 1964, when his exile in Uruguay prevented him, along with many other politicians, from continuing to dine at the Bife de Ouro.

Zweig and the Princess of the Sea

In 1946, the same year that the construction of the Annexe was begun, American impresario and producer Wallace Downey planned to open a new nightclub called the "Copacabana" in New York. He commissioned a song from João de Barro and Altino Ribeiro to promote the nightclub, and although it was a good offer, it took the composers too long, in true *carioca* fashion, to complete the song; it was only finished long after the nightclub had been inaugurated. Irritated, Downey turned the song down, and the two composers were left with no choice but to launch it in Brazil, where *Copacabana* became a resounding success.

Copacabana, Princess of the Sea,
In the morning
You are life full of song.
And in the evening,
When the sun goes down,
You always leave us
Melancholy.

Copacabana,
The sea, that endless crooner,
Upon kissing you
Became lost in love
And today lives murmuring:
I will always love
Only you, Copacabana.

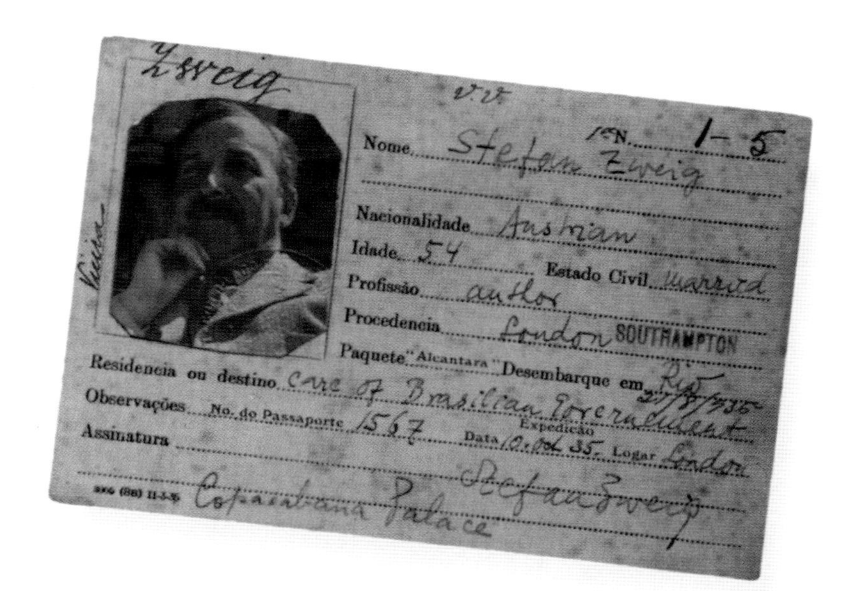

Zweig

Nome Stefan Zweig N. 1-5
Nacionalidade Austrian
Idade 54 Estado Civil married
Profissão author
Procedencia London SOUTHAMPTON
Paquete "Alcantara" Desembarque em Rio
Residencia ou destino Care of Brasilian Government
Observações No. do Passaporte 1567 Expedição Data 10. Oct. 35. Logar London
Assinatura Stefan Zweig
Copacabana Palace

Writer Stefan Zweig (above) was an acknowledged admirer of Copacabana, which he considered to have the most beautiful beach in the world

"If Copacabana does not represent the heart of Rio, it does, at least, its lungs. But for all its beauty one thing is symbolic: whether standing or sitting on this beach facing the sea, we really have Rio at our backs, as this avenue looks towards Europe."
Stefan Zweig

In 1941, five years before this song became consecrated as Copacabana's anthem, Austrian writer Stefan Zweig had already become infected with this spirit of collective reverence. In his book *Brasil, país do futuro* [Brazil, Country of the Future], he dedicated a lengthy passage to the mysteries and sensuality of Copacabana. "We are merely at another beginning, at one of the many beginnings which this city always offers, in such a surprising fashion," he wrote. "You have merely to traverse two streets and one tunnel cut through solid rock to find yourself suddenly on the beach of Copacabana, far more beautiful than Nice or Miami. We are on perhaps the most beautiful beach in the world. Incredible as it may seem, in just five minutes of travel, from Rio to Rio, we are on the edge of another sea, another climate, another temperature, as if we had travelled for several hours. And the sea we had seen on Avenida Beira-Mar is, in effect, different, as it is the water of a bay that is almost entirely enclosed. It is undoubtedly a sea, but a subdued, attenuated sea without the strength to raise furious waves and, in spite of its size, showing no clear tidal activity. But in Copacabana suddenly our wind-blown visage stares directly into the Atlantic, and we know and sense that nothing but thousands of miles of this immense ocean separate us from Europe and Africa. Powerful, foamy green waves, Neptune's white-maned horses, throw themselves upon the wide, clear, splendid beach. The sound of the waves resonates in your ears and so strong is their beating upon the beach, so intense is the breath of the Atlantic giant, that from the pulverized water emanates iodine and salt. The air is so rich in ozone that

many people accustomed to a milder, gentler atmosphere cannot stand living on this beach that is always so clamorous, in this atmosphere so saturated with humidity. But how refreshing! After a five-minute drive, ambient temperature is four or five degrees lower. Of the hundreds of secrets of this city, those which only a long-time resident would know, one is the fact that here, from one corner to the next, the temperatures differ sharply. In the same area a back street may be warm while the front one is cool, the street to the right breezy while one to the left is calm, and all because they are at given angles to the direction of the sea breeze, or because the breeze cannot reach them at all, blocked by a hill. Copacabana beach is a luxurious beach. It has a magnificent hotel, excellent bars, one of which features a gypsy band, a gambling casino, wide sidewalks and, above all, its own customs – which are somewhat un-Brazilian. Only in Copacabana does one see, as in European and North American summer resorts, girls wearing men's trousers and men in sports shirts with no jackets. On this avenue there are bars with tables in the open air. There are no shops and no trucks pass by, as this beach is given over exclusively to luxury, to pleasure, to sport, to recreation, to colour and to the pleasures of the flesh and of the eyes. This avenue is, when all is said and done, a kind of luxury bathing cabin on a gigantic beach, which on some days attracts 100 thousand people without becoming overcrowded. At times one has the impression that this beach does not actually belong to the city of Rio, that it, in a manner similar (but more grandiose) to what happened in Nice, was artificially attached to a large city of business, of activity, for the pleasure of foreigners and high-rollers, and only gradually penetrated into the life and the essence of the city. In fact, for twenty years there were some timid little houses that dared to stand on the dunes. But, once the automobile was invented, whole city blocks sprang up in Copacabana at an astonishing speed. With the same facility that in Vienna one goes to the Prater or in Paris to the Bois de Boulogne, today one goes to Copacabana, whereas previously this had been an excursion, almost a voyage. If Copacabana does not represent the heart of Rio, it does, at least, its lungs. But for all its beauty one thing is symbolic: whether standing or sitting on this beach facing the sea, we really have Rio at our backs, as this avenue looks towards Europe. It is as European as Avenida Rio Branco was thirty years ago, and it is a known fact that more foreign-

ers and travellers prefer to stay on Avenida Atlântica than do the true *cariocas*, who feel less at home there, and more like guests." Today, without a doubt, Zweig would have to revise many of his impressions and conclusions. On Avenida Atlântica, although commerce is still centred on bars with chairs on the sidewalks, trucks are no longer prohibited, especially those loaded with coconuts, thousands of coconuts whose water, cool and slightly sweet, is one of the *carioca*'s passions. Living on the seaside is also no longer the exclusive privilege of foreigners, and today on summer weekends Copacabana receives almost ten times as many bathers as the 100 thousand that so impressed the writer. Since the sea was pushed back in the 1960's to widen the beach as well as to allow for additional traffic lanes on Avenida Atlântica, there continues to be room for all comers on a sunny day, but not, alas, "without becoming overcrowded." Nevertheless, over half a century later, the beach is still a special place dedicated "to pleasure, to sport, to recreation, to colour and to the pleasures of the flesh and of the eyes."

Citizen Orson

In late 1942, Orson Welles came to the Copacabana that Zweig described. At 26, he had already directed one of the greatest films in movie history, *Citizen Kane*. The Second World War was in full swing, and Welles had come to Brazil to make a film, as part of the "Good Neighbours Policy." This American public relations programme, coordinated by future vice-president Nelson Rockefeller, was designed to win over Latin American support for the Allies. Brazil was under the Vargas dictatorship, and the Government looked upon Welles's visit as an opportunity to propagate a favourable image of the country abroad. The film project made its way through the diplomatic channels, and Welles was offered the assistance of an American executive from RKO and a Brazilian representative of the DIP, the Government's Press and Propaganda Department, an agency which was also responsible for the censorship of all communications. Washington ostensibly supported Welles's work. It was no coincidence that the director, his 22 technicians and three tons of equipment arrived on the same airplane sent to Brazil to fetch the American delegation, which was at the Rio de Janeiro Conference negotiating agreements for the defense of the Americas. So as not to miss the free ride, Welles moved his schedule up, leaving two movies unfinished in the United States, *The Magnificent Ambersons* and *Journey into Fear*, which he was directing simultaneously. For the first few days of his eight-month stay at the Copacabana Palace, Welles followed

Orson Welles arrived in Brazil in 1942 to make an official film for the U.S. Government, but changed his mind halfway through and produced "It's All True," in which he tells, among other stories, the saga of four fishermen from Ceará

A guest at the Copa, Welles became famous for his drinking sprees. On one occasion, after a fight with Dolores Del Rio (above), he hurled furniture from his apartment into the pool. Welles (opposite) between singers Ademilde Fonseca and Elizete Cardoso at the hotel's carnival ball

the well-behaved itinerary of an official guest, gathering images of elegant parties and the popular carnival. However, as he became more familiar with the city, going up into the hills, frequenting the lower-class dance halls, drinking cheap sugar-cane liquor in corner bars and visiting the red-light district, his basic premise for the film began to change. Rather than make an institutional semi-documentary, he decided to tell the story of samba, with all its social implications and without a fixed script. Reactions were swift. The RKO executive began sending reports back to the studio wherein he accused Welles of filming "a bunch of monkeys," while the DIP man insisted, in vain, that the director include post-card shots of Rio – Sugar Loaf Mountain and the Statue of Christ – in the film. Welles, unheeding, alternated between short bursts of filming and lots of women and boozing. He even created a drink called Samba-in-Berlin, a mixture of Coca-Cola and the local *cachaça*, which became popular. He also learned to speak Portuguese in no time, and proved himself a keen student in the tambourine lessons he was receiving from the percussionist Caboré, a member of the National Radio Orchestra. At this stage, Welles had in mind that other, unscripted film, so he changed the original conciliatory title of *Alô, amigos* [Hello, Friends] to the intriguing *It's All True*. On his frequent drinking sprees, Welles found himself at the centre of several scandals. On one occasion, for instance, he hurled furniture from his window into the hotel swimming pool, enraged after an international phone call from his girlfriend, Dolores Del Rio. The actress had complained not only about Welles's prolonged absence, but also about reports of his compromising behaviour in Rio. The Copacabana Palace, however, continued to give Welles special treatment. *Maître d'hôtel* Fery Wünsch relates in his memoirs that one night the American phoned down to the front desk complaining that the water had run out in the middle of his shower. After a diplomatic explanation of the circumstances that exposed the denizens of Rio to this common inconvenience, Wünsch sent bottles of mineral water up to Welles's apartment so that he could finish his bath. On the following day, a tropical rainstorm burst over Rio. Once again, the telephone rang at the front desk. Welles, calling Wünsch by the nickname he had given him, bellowed, "Fritz, I need to place a call downtown, and I can't get a phone line!" An attempt to explain that the telephone network was down due to flooding resulted in an order

RADIO

for Wünsch to ascend immediately to the American's room, where Orson Welles, dishevelled and furious, shouted, "When I want a bath, there's no water. When I want to use the phone, I can't because the lines are full of water. You tell me, Fritz, which one of us is crazy?" When the budget for the film was nearly depleted (500 thousand dollars, a hefty sum at the time), Welles caught wind of an exploit that had occurred the previous year. Four fishermen had sailed from Fortaleza to Rio on a native Northeastern masted raft. With no navigation instruments they sailed eighteen hundred miles in 61 days to present their labour complaints to President Vargas. Impressed, Welles decided to include the story in his film and commissioned a script from Edmar Morel, a journalist who had written several articles about the adventure at the time. The director and his 22 assistants, who already occupied 18 rooms in the Copacabana Palace, now found their numbers increased by 20 Brazilians, among them writers, musicians, announcers, technicians and artists (such as Grande Otelo), all being paid in dollars. The fishermen were brought to Rio to re-enact their odyssey before the cameras. The day after their arrival, "Jacaré" (Alligator), the group's leader, was drowned off the Barra da Tijuca when the production's launch executed a sudden maneuver which caused the fisherman's raft to capsize. The tragedy annihilated the project. RKO immediately published a communication in the newspapers declaring themselves no longer responsible for Orson Welles's expenditures. At the same time, the DIP agency worked on the news media to reinforce the assertion, originally made by the American press, that Welles was a communist. In arrears with his bills at the Copa and owing his employees, the director sold part of his assets in the United States to pay off all his debts in Brazil. The filming of *It's All True* would not be resumed, and the film's negatives disappeared. Nearly half a century later, in 1985, they were found in a Paramount archive, stored in 309 sealed cans. The work was finally produced by Richard Wilson, a member of the team that accompanied Welles to Brazil, and was shown for the first time at the opening of the New York Film Festival in 1990.

Hollywood was here

The "Good Neighbours Policy" also had its Brazilian counterpart. If Orson Welles, Walt Disney and others came to Rio to reinforce the American image here, the DIP relied in Hollywood on the services of a man who painted an alluring picture of *carioca* life, and then invited celebrities to experience it. This man was Jorginho Guinle, whose name was to become bound to the history of the Copacabana Palace almost as inseparably as was that of his uncle Otávio, the hotel's founder. Jorginho, easygoing heir to a great fortune, lover of jazz and beautiful women, moved from France to the United States on the eve of the Second World War. At that time he had no plans for the future, but three years later he was nominated Brazilian representative of the American Office for South American Affairs, and consequently enjoyed free access to the executives and stars of the largest studios in the cinema world. In his memoirs, published in 1997, Jorginho Guinle confessed that his connection to the family that owned the Copacabana Palace opened more doors than the possession of a government emissary's credentials. The hotel's fame, born of the film *Flying Down to Rio*, was the best calling card available – and Jorginho used it liberally. Free from financial worries and faithful to the principle that "life is the pursuit of pleasure," this former Collège de France philosophy student embarked in the 1940's on a career as an international playboy. Dividing his time between Los Angeles and New York, Guinle's lifestyle rivaled that of

Walt Disney's Zé Carioca, supporting the "Good Neighbours Policy"

Jorge Guinle (above, with Dolores Guinle, made a name for himself as an international playboy, rivalling Porfirio Rubirosa and Ali Khan

Porfirio Rubirosa and Ali Khan. Jorginho's official mission (an excuse to live in paradise, safe from the call of military service) consisted of searching through Hollywood films for scenes that might harm the friendly relations between Brazil and the United States. If on the one hand his zeal did not prevent countless bandits in American productions from evincing a wish to live in Rio after having swindled or murdered their enemies on the screen, it did provide Jorginho in 1944 with the privilege of a first-hand meeting with the character Zé Carioca, created by Walt Disney for his cartoon *The Three Caballeros*. Among his more successful ventures, Guinle managed to avoid cinematographic errors such as the insertion of Rio's Statue of Christ up among the icy peaks of the Andes. Jorginho's friendships and love affairs were invaluable to the international reputation of the Copacabana Palace, the inevitable destination of those the high-flyer lured to Brazil. This interchange, initiated for political reasons during the Second World War, intensified in the following decades. In 1954, Jorginho brought to Brazil the largest delegation he had ever managed to organize in the U.S., "without having to pay a single dollar in fees." The group brought together names such as Errol Flynn, Joan Fontaine, Mary Pickford, Rhonda Fleming, John Derek, Cesar Romero, Walter Pidgeon, Glenn Ford, Ann Miller and June Haver. This last, who had worked with Carmen Miranda in *The Gang's All Here*, was on her first international voyage after three years in the convent to which she had retired after deciding to abandon cinema. In Rio, the actress began a love affair with Fred MacMurray, her travel companion, whom she married a few months later. Also part of the delegation was the eternal gangster Edward G. Robinson, with a fat cigar perpetually between his fingers. One sunny morning, poolside, he became the centre of attention as he haggled with marchand Jean Boghicci for the purchase of a painting by Paulo Pedro Leal. This naïf painter, the son of slaves, exhibited his work on Rio's pavements, where he was discovered by the marchand. Robinson and Boghicci were both Rumanian and, talking in their native tongue, closed the sale for fifty dollars, ten times more than the artist (a mute witness to the deal) was accustomed to receiving for his paintings. Jorginho Guinle would make roughly thirty trips to Hollywood between 1957 and 1962, always handing out invitations that were increasingly well received. The 1950's at the Copacabana Palace were

G A R Ô T A S

Fazendeiros no Paraná, os pais de Betinho
e Fernando estão preocupados com os
dois soltos aqui no Rio, justamente no Carnaval...

marked not only by this constant presence of American artists, but also by the hey-day of the carnival balls. The history of Rio de Janeiro relates that in the beginning, carnival festivities were held only in hotels and did not welcome common people as guests. The first carnival ball on record in Rio was the "Night of the Masks." Inspired by the carnival in Venice, it was held in the Hotel Itália, near Praça Tiradentes, in 1853, to the sound of waltzes, polkas and mazurkas. Only six decades later, in 1916, a Portuguese shoemaker, José Nogueira de Azevedo Paredes (Zé Pereira) paraded around the downtown area beating a drum, attracting a large following, thereby originating the definitive and true street carnival. A few months after its inauguration, in February 1924, the Copacabana Palace started the tra-

"Conheci uma espanhola"
"Natural da Catalunha"

The Copa ball, which competed with the Municipal ball was the most sought-after in Brazil, showcased actresses such as Ilka Soares (above) and Mexican comedian Cantinflas (below, to the right of Dolores Guinle)

dition of holding its carnival ball on a Saturday, an initiative that was eagerly taken up. In order to participate in the "First Empire Ball" in 1933, *carioca* society ordered from Europe period costumes as sumptuous as those worn in the court of Napoleon. Two years later, the demand for tables had increased to such an extent that the hotel had to pay off the Casino concessionaires for the right to suspend gaming for three days and occupy their salons. In time, reservations for the ball could only be honoured if they were made a year in advance. Until it was discontinued in 1973, the Copa ball shared with the Municipal ball the status of most vied-for and elegant in Brazil. Costume parades were all the rage, and with them names such as Clóvis Bornay, Evandro de Castro Lima and Zacharias do Rêgo Monteiro, the eternal Pierrot. With each passing year the creations they exhibited became increasingly expensive and fantastical. The masses followed these parades closely, transmitted live by TV stations and always livened up by competitors exchanging catty remarks and complaining about the jury. On the night of the ball, traffic-jamming crowds would gather along Avenida Copacabana and at the entrance to the hotel, eager to see the flourish of celebrities and costumes. Newspapers reported on the décor and scenery in the salons. Among the themes, over the years, were "Harlequin Trio;" "Rio, Always Rio;" "Batucada" and "Old Rio." This last, in 1965, was so grandiose that it set a public record by gathering six thousand people.

Two attractions at the Copa: Carmélia Alves's show at the Midnight Club, broadcast live by Rádio Nacional, and the fashions created by Dior for the Bangu label

Bohemia, art and elegance

Copacabana was, as we have seen, a neighbourhood where taboos and prejudices did not last long. Residents cultivated an "American way of life," and increasingly gave in to the novelties of this lifestyle. Among other things, they saw the first fast-food snack bar in the country, as well as "self-service stores," the precursors of supermarkets. These modernizations did not, however, affect the neighbourhood's great hotel, which remained faithful to its classical European style, even while risking the introduction of "Americanized" innovations, as it did in the 1950's with the opening of the Midnight Club. With a menu that became famous for its "Midnight Hash" (a dish that became the staple of elegant Rio's night owls), the club marked an era in *carioca* bohemia, cultivating a legion of devoted clients who made it their meeting place for the last drinks of the evening. To reserve a table one had to be in cahoots with the *maîtres d'*. Those who were so privileged enjoyed an environment in which one could chat and at the same time listen to quality music, such as Dick Farney at the piano, crooners Luís Bandeira and Helena de Lima and the so-called "little bands" led by Copinha, Steve Bernard and Zacharias. Sometimes, zeal for the intimacy of the atmosphere would prompt Otávio Guinle to discreetly ask the drummers to contain their enthusiastic performances. Artists with other abilities were also presented in the nightclub, as in the case of Italian illusionist "Doctor Giovanni," who impressed with his

ability to pick the pockets of the men in the audience – their wallets always returned, to applause, at the end of the show. Such was his technique that he gave lessons to the police, training agents in charge of apprehending pick-pockets in the streets. In the wee hours, during the Rádio Nacional broadcast of a programme called *Ritmos da Panair*, the public at large heard the music live from the nightclub. The late-night audience following transformed Murilo Neri, the programme presenter, into one of the most familiar voices on radio and later on Brazilian TV. If nights at the Copa were ruled by musicals in the Golden Room and nightcaps in the Midnight Club, the days also had plenty to offer. Musical Afternoons in the Green Room, at the entrance to the Annexe, gathered society ladies together to the sound of Freddy's piano for charity benefits and *thés de tête*, where the latest creations in feminine millinery were presented. Fashion shows had always enjoyed great prestige at the Copacabana Palace, which for years was the setting for the Bangu parades, the most celebrated of them all. Conceived in 1951 to promote Brazilian-made fabrics, they marked the beginning of the *haute couture* industry in the country, until then the exclusive province of French stylists. Determined to exalt the status of the printed cottons they produced in a Rio suburb, the Bangu factory went as far as Europe to contract famous fashion designer Jacques Fath, who, at his castle in

Maestro Copinha's orchestra backs Carmélia Alves at the microphone (left) and a scene from the Miss Elegant Bangu pageant, featuring the most elegant society demoiselles (above)

Fernando de Barros apresenta

Tonia Carrero

em

AMANHÃ,
SE NÃO CHOVER...

comédia de Henrique Pongetti

com

PAULO AUTRAN

VERA NUNES

ARMANDO COUTO

DIREÇÃO DE ZIEMBINSKI. CENARIOS E FIGURINOS DE LAZLO MEITNER

TEATRO COPACABANA

AR REFRIGERADO

The state-of-the-art Copacabana Theatre (above, right) staged plays such as "Amanhã se não chover," with Tônia Carrero (above, left) and "Flor de cactus," designed by Napoleão Muniz Freire (opposite)

Corbeville, designed models for a sumptuous show of Bangu fashions in 1952. In subsequent years, Hubert de Givenchy and Christian Dior also produced designs for the Bangu griffe. The collections of formal and casual women's clothing were launched at the Copacabana Palace, and the shows, broadcast on the radio, became a national attraction. Organized fan clubs followed the selection of Miss Elegant Bangu, a competition featuring society girls representing the most exclusive clubs in Brazil. The winner received two thousand dollars, samples of Brazilian fabrics and a complete wardrobe to show off on the catwalks of Paris, in addition to the trip itself. Bangu, whose styles were copied by ever more competitors, put an end to the fashion shows in 1960, having manifestly attained their original objective. There were fashion, fun, bohemia and worldliness galore, but the Copacabana Palace was also an important centre for culture, housing successive art exhibitions (264 watercoloured etchings by Cândido Portinari graced the walls of the hotel's bedrooms), recitals and concerts. And from 1949, it also had the Copacabana Theatre, the largest in the area. It was the successor to the old Copacabana Theatre-Casino, a Louis Seize-style salon where for 25 years troupes from other countries had held centre stage. The new Copacabana Theatre soon became known for welcoming unusual Brazilian theatre, in a market still heavily dominated by foreign companies

Discos
PIAF
EL CID

Scenes from Henriette Morineau's 1953 "Catarina da Rússia" (top) and "Um deus dormiu lá em casa" (above) which marked the début of the hugely successful Tônia Carrero and Paulo Autran artistic partnership, 1949

Fernanda Montenegro on stage: with Henriette Morineau in "Mulheres feias," 1953 (top) and with Sérgio Britto in "O mambembe," 1959-60 (above); the design for her costume (below)

and European actors. The new facility, designed along the most modern concepts of the day, combined state-of-the-art technical resources with sober elegance. Seating 500, the theatre boasted seats clad in green leather, walls panelled in pale wood and a marble-floored foyer. Upon entering, one waited for the programme to begin by imbibing at the sophisticated bar or gazing at display windows carrying the latest offerings from jewellers and designers. Attendants in white gloves and impeccable uniforms collected entrance tickets, showing people to their numbered seats and taking hats and coats. Thanks to the air-conditioning, unheard-of in *carioca* theatres, ladies were able to show off their fur coats, normally left to hang in cold storage at Casa Sibéria. The first play to be staged was *A mulher do próximo* [The Neighbour's Wife], by Abílio Pereira de Almeida. It marked the debut as a professional actor of the young lawyer Paulo Autran, one of the many artistic revelations of the Copacabana Theatre. Three months later, now as leading man in another first showing, (*Um deus dormiu lá em casa* [A God Slept at our Place], by Guilherme Figueiredo), Autran discovered Tônia Carrero, the partner with whom he was to form the most successful couple in Brazilian theatre. Previously, the gorgeous young gym teacher had attracted attention for her ravishing beauty around the Copacabana Palace swimming pool, especially when the foreign race-car drivers were at the hotel, in town to race the Gavea Circuit, one of the World Automobile Championship tracks. Sharing the stage with the musical revues (common during intervals between seasons), almost fifty companies were featured at the Copacabana Theatre. Of them all, the most frequently seen was Henriette Morineau's Artistas Unidos, responsible for 27 productions and for the discovery of many first-rate Brazilian actors and actresses. This was the case in 1953 with Fernanda Montenegro, who, at 23, received the title of Revelation of the Year for her part in *Mulheres feias* [Ugly Women], the first of many awards with which the critics would fête her throughout her career. A stream of important figures in Brazilian theatre passed through the fifteen dressing rooms of the Copacabana Theatre, among them Procópio Ferreira, Cacilda Becker, Paulo Gracindo, André Villon, Cecil Thiré, Cleyde Yaconis, Eva Wilma, Glauce Rocha, Jardel Filho, Juca de Oliveira, Nicette Bruno, Nathalia Timberg, Paulo Goulart, Jorge Dória, Sérgio Britto, Ítalo Rossi, Maria Della Costa, Yolanda Cardoso, Walmor

Chagas, Yoná Magalhães, Zilka Salaberry and Ziembinsky. With these and other actors, productions frequently achieved record attendance and outstanding box-office results, thereby inspiring ever more ambitious productions. This fortuitous sequence was to be interrupted by disaster in the second half of 1953, when long queues were forming to buy tickets for *Mulheres feias.* On the morning of August 10, the explosion of a light bulb ignited a fire which destroyed the Copacabana Theatre, the Golden Room (where American singer Dorothy Dandridge had star-billing), the Midnight Club and the salons of the defunct Casino. Also lost were the scenery and wardrobes for more than ten plays, taking Artistas Unidos to the brink of bankruptcy. "It was impossible to believe what was happening," recalls Fernanda Montenegro. "Otávio Guinle looked after the hotel as if he were the captain of a transatlantic luxury liner. Nobody could believe that the palace was being reduced to ashes." In spite of the size of the fire, there was no panic among the guests. Newspapers of the day relate that they filled the tables at the poolside bar and, fortified by tea and drinks, watched the drama unfold. The reception desk of the Copacabana Palace continued to function normally, enabling, for example, Princess Ragnhild of Norway and all her voluminous baggage to depart on schedule. Fire-fighting efforts were hampered by a lack of water in nearby hydrants, so gúests united against the blaze and tossed ineffectual streams of water over the fire with buckets filled from taps in the Annexe apartments. Five hours later, the fire was finally put out by water pumped out of the swimming pool through the firemen's hoses. While there were no fatalities, the hotel sustained enormous damage. It wasn't until late 1955 that the facilities damaged by the fire reopened to the public. The Copacabana Theatre, restored to its original design, was re-inaugurated with *Diálogo das carmelitas* [Dialogue of

The Copacabana Theatre boasted a novelty for its time: air conditioning, which allowed the ladies to show off their fur coats

Some fifty companies played in the theatre, the most frequent being Henriette Morineau's Artistas Unidos

the Carmelites]. Thanks to this drama by George Bernanos, Artistas Unidos was able to resume its interrupted series of successes. In the 39 following years, the theatre hosted hundreds of plays and recitals and reigned as one of the city's most established cultural arenas. In 1994, after a season's run of *Desejo* [Desire] (with Vera Fischer, Juca de Oliveira and Guilherme Fontes), the theatre closed down once again, this time for lengthy construction work required to reinforce its foundations. Approval for this work by official heritage preservation agencies is still awaited.

Linda go home

During the 1940's and '50's, Rio's élite moved in and took up, once and for all, the "Copacabana way of life." Spacious homes on verdant plots in residential districts of the city were exchanged for far smaller apartments on Copacabana beach, at the expense of both space and privacy. Copacabana was a new status symbol, and it managed to welcome all levels of the social strata, democratically accommodating the high society, the upper-middle-class, and the first shanty-dwellers of the neighbourhood. Anti-heroes such as James Dean and Marlon Brando, arrogant individualists, began to replace the well-mannered and patriotic heroes that Hollywood had so patiently moulded. Faithful to the new style, young men in Copacabana dressed in stifling leather jackets. The girls, who favoured magazines devoted to movie stars, often saw the same film over and over again in order to learn how to dress and behave. Some memorable incidents from the world of cinema took place quite near these *carioca* fans. For example, there was Ava Gardner's visit in 1954. In Rio on an itinerary established by United Artists to promote the film *The Barefoot Contessa*, Ava was expelled from the Hotel Glória at two o'clock in the morning for going on a destructive drunken rampage in her room. In the face of this embarrassing situation, which hit all the headlines, the Copacabana Palace was asked to put the actress up – which Otávio Guinle agreed to with some trepidation. At her new address, Ava caused much commotion, but did

Ava Gardner (above) and Ginger Rogers (below): two Hollywood stars who created shock waves during their stays at the Copa

The hotel and its famous guests: Ava Gardner (above) could not disguise her unhappiness at the end of her marriage to Frank Sinatra; Anita Ekberg (below) exchanged slaps and kisses with Anthony Steel; Ginger Rogers and Elaine Stewart went dancing (opposite, top), and Yul Brynner declared his preference for the dusky "carioca" girls (below)

not take part in any new scandals. After having switched rooms three times on the same day due to a bewildering variety of demands, she finally accepted the hotel's invitation to the Midnight Club, where she appeared escorted by Brazil's most famous social columnists, Ibrahim Sued and Jacinto de Thormes. There, Ava, in spite of enjoying her first moments of relaxation in Rio, fell to weeping whenever the orchestra played tunes from the repertoire of her husband, Frank Sinatra, from whom she was recently estranged. The following year Elaine Stewart and Ginger Rogers would garner the city's attention. As mentioned previously, Elaine visited Carmen Miranda in 1955, during the latter's convalescence at the Copa. The American artist was also in regular attendance at the Midnight Club, fuelling rumours that she was in love with Ibrahim Sued, in whose company she was seen on a number of occasions. The rumours, which went so far as to speculate on a possible marriage, were unexpectedly interrupted: suffering from severe abdominal pains, Elaine was rushed to the Strangers' Hospital. Acute appendicitis was suspected, and Ibrahim even imagined a possible pregnancy. But the physician who attended the actress, Ivo Pitanguy (later to attain world fame as a plastic surgeon), recalls that she remained under observation only one night. Nevertheless, the newspapers announced that Elaine had thanked the employees of the Copacabana Palace for the care lavished upon her during her confinement of almost one month to the hotel, "while recovering from an operation." Briefer and less fraught than Elaine Stewart's stay was Ginger Rogers's visit to Rio. Besides participating in the Copa and Municipal carnival balls, Ginger also visited art galleries. On one such incursion, she bought a painting by Guignard. The picture, which would be worth over 100 thousand dollars today, was sent off to the United States and never seen again. During that same year, the Copacabana Palace hosted other famous actresses of the day, such as Barbara Rush, Annie Francis and Jeanne Crain. In 1956 Susan Hayward arrived, unleashing a furor when invited to a special audience with President Juscelino Kubitschek, her declared fan. Movie stars were not the only guests responsible for the permanent international visibility of the hotel. Royalty and heads of state from all over the world stayed there, and even when they did not, they still used the Copa's facilities and services. This happened in 1957, when Portugal's President Craveiro Lopes came to Brazil. He took

up residence at the Laranjeiras Palace, but it was the Copacabana Palace that was responsible for providing all the infra-structure the visitor required, from bed linen to kitchen materials, and even a *maître d'* and a butler. Also in 1957 the hotel hosted the entire delegation sent by Hollywood to the Punta del Este Cinema Festival. Unfortunately, it rained copiously every single day of the week that the group spent in Rio. But, while there was no sun, there were still high-jinks aplenty to entertain the press. The main attractions were the monumental fights between Swedish beauty Anita Ekberg and her husband, British actor Anthony Steel. The upshot of the frequent slaps and infrequent kisses the couple had been exchanging since Uruguay was that Anita suddenly abandoned the group and flew to Stockholm. On the following day, after having given interviews declaring himself repentant, and locking himself in his apartment to drink two bottles of gin, Steel left for Los Angeles, denying any possibility of divorce. Besides this tempestuous couple, the celebrity-studded delegation included Lana Turner (who had a crying jag in Rio upon learning that millionaire Howard Hughes, whom she was expecting to marry, had just married Jean Peters), Ann Miller, Van Heflin and Yul Brynner. This last, widely believed to be the son of a Rumanian gypsy and a Swiss with Mongolian origins, was a great believer in the miscegenation of races. He charmed the *cariocas* when he declared himself enamored of "deeply bronzed brunettes." This description fitted Iracema, a crooner in Bené Nunes's band, with whom the actor had a brief flirtation. Soon after the departure of the Hollywood delegation, the Copa welcomed Louis Armstrong. The singer and trumpet player was the star attraction at a series of performances in the city, including one at the Maracanãzinho gymnasium, which was thronged with spectators. A man of insatiable thirst, Armstrong always carried an enormous canteen on his shoulder, which his manager swore contained only water. However, the intense heat of Rio soon had "Satchmo" securely hooked on ice-cold beer. His friendliness and talent were not the only qualities that captivated the Brazilians. At a time when racial discrimination was rampant in the United States and also had many undeclared sympathizers in Rio, Armstrong held a reception at the American embassy and made a point of inviting coloured artists and football players, who had in common the fact that none of them had ever set foot there before. Broken

romances also helped to write the history of the Copacabana Palace. Figuring in one such episode was Linda Christian, ex-wife of Tyrone Power. Better known for her rich husbands than for her acting, Linda had lived out a torrid romance with Baby Pignatari in the United States. The year was 1958, and Baby had put an end to the affair. The actress came out to Rio to attempt a reconciliation, but in doing so gave the millionaire an opportunity to make it unequivocally clear that it was all over. Cruelly, Baby united his cronies from the Clube dos Cafajestes for a unique demonstration in front of the Copacabana Palace. On hearing her name called from the street, Linda appeared at her window and was surprised to see a band of ruffians (some of them contracted for the occasion) brandishing posters reading "Linda go home!" and setting off fireworks. Deeply humiliated, the actress took the first flight home to the United States, where the incident was widely publicized, depressing her even further. The coarseness of his treatment of Linda got Baby Pignatari banned from the Copacabana Palace – the ban was repealed some time later when the playboy sent an apology to Otávio Guinle, together with a truckload of roses, an act of respect he had been incapable of affording Linda Christian. The press savoured these celebrity visits with enthusiasm, the saucier the better. In 1959, Jayne Mansfield, then at the height of her popularity, was in Rio with her husband, Mickey Hargitay, a bodybuilder who had won the Mr. America title. Jayne nearly paralyzed the Copa carnival ball when the strap of her straining dress broke free, threatening to expose over forty inches of the charms that had earned the actress the nickname of "The Bust." Reporter Guimarães Padilha of the *Tribuna da Imprensa* was accused of having precipitated the "accident," but he strenuously denied having unzipped Jayne's dress. During the mêlée, Hargitay's imposing physique was not enough to deter the advance of some of the bolder men in the crowd. When he realized what was happening, Mr. America covered his wife with his jacket, protecting her

Linda Christian and Baby Pignatari (right), players in a bizarre spectacle at the doors of the hotel

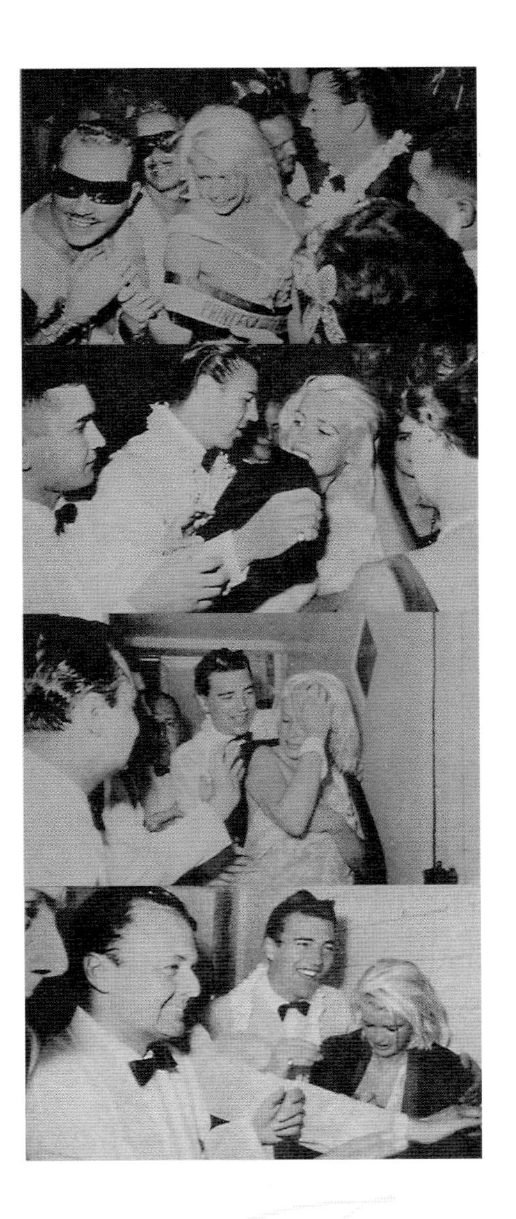

Jayne Mansfield starred in an unusual scene at the Copa ball: a strap on her gown broke, to the delight of her fans and the chagrin of her husband, who tried at all costs to conceal the actress' ample virtues

from flash bulbs and prying eyes while they beat a retreat from the party. The episode dominated that carnival's headlines. Two days later, at the Municipal ball, the crowd chorused an appeal for Jayne to take off her blouse, this time voluntarily. In a friendly gesture, the actress responded by throwing her shoes to the fans instead.

CHAPTER FIVE

Farewell to the Capital

Night and Day

To the Beat of the Bossa-Nova

Exoticism and a tropical climate were not the only attractions on offer to the growing swarm of *cariocas* and tourists who sought Copacabana's enchantment. During the late 1950's the area lured visitors with something other than beaches, bars, countless nightclubs and good restaurants. This something was the unexpected – the surprise of discovery, of unusual happenings, which as often as not become the norm. This is what happened in an alley known as the "Beco das Garrafas" [Bottle Alley], near the back of the Copacabana Palace. Two nightclubs, the Little Club and the Baccarat, stepped into the history of contemporary music when they hosted the first public performances of young artists such as João Gilberto, Tom Jobim, Roberto Menescal and Nara Leão, pioneers of the bossa-nova. The strains of this new style, which had already been heard in some of Copacabana's more deluxe apartments, reflected the tastes and sensibilities of the layers of social classes that coexisted harmoniously in the neighbourhood. Never before had Brazilian popular music managed to express itself in a manner so modern and free from those influences and caricatures that marked, for example, the Carmen Miranda phenomenon. The rhythm and personality of the bossa-nova crossed frontiers and brought international fame to some of its exponents. The truly public debut of the bossa-nova occurred in the Golden Room in 1961, when

singer Silvinha Telles and the Trio Irakitan performed the classic *Samba de uma nota só* [*One-Note Samba*] in a scene in the musical *Skindô*. A few years later, the Jazz & Bossa Club (founded by Ricardo Cravo Albim), united the two styles of music with the voices of Leny Andrade, Tuca and Chico Buarque de Holanda, together with Tom Jobin (piano), Victor Assis Brasil (sax), Hélio Delmiro and Luís Bonfá (guitar), and others. The group held Saturday afternoon sessions at the Midnight Club and lived off monthly contributions collected with great difficulty by Nis Skou, a Norwegian executive infatuated with the bossa-nova. In 1964, their extreme insolvency led to the Jazz & Bossa's eviction, whereupon they began to wander from one nightclub to another until the group finally dissolved. Rio de Janeiro's delights created an entertaining and stimulating atmosphere, apparent on all levels of cultural output, and the *cariocas* suffered a violent blow when the capital of the Republic was transferred to Brasília. The lengthy process of Rio's political and economic depletion began then, and its effects are still being felt today. The city had been the centre of power since colonial days, but as of April 21, 1960, it faced losses and reversals that did not even spare its official name, which became the "State of Guanabara." This legal change, decreed by President Kubitschek, would only be repealed in 1974, when Rio gained the status of municipality. Although the administrative act that transferred the capital occurred at the beginning of the 1960's, the move effectively took almost ten years. More so than the ministries and Federal agencies, the diplomatic corps, responsible for much of the city's social life, resisted the change of address until the early 1970's. In February of 1960, during Rio's last carnival as the capital, the Copa ball hosted actresses Kim Novak (then at the peak of her career), Zsa Zsa Gabor and Linda Darnell. Immediately upon her arrival, Kim Novak declared her support for the Cuban Revolution and her admiration for Fidel Castro to the newspaper *Última Hora*. The interview had international repercussions and forever chilled the star's relations with the American studios. This was not, however, the only political statement she would make during her visit. Eager to mix with the people dancing in the streets, she left the Municipal ball in full swing and went to Jorginho Guinle's home to change out of her elegant gown into something more fitting. For her new costume she wore a dark wig and loose clothing purpose-

It was in Copacabana, in the Beco das Garrafas, that the first chords of the bossa-nova were heard at performances by João Gilberto (above, with Lena Horne) and Tom Jobim (below, with Chico Buarque and Cynara and Cybelle)

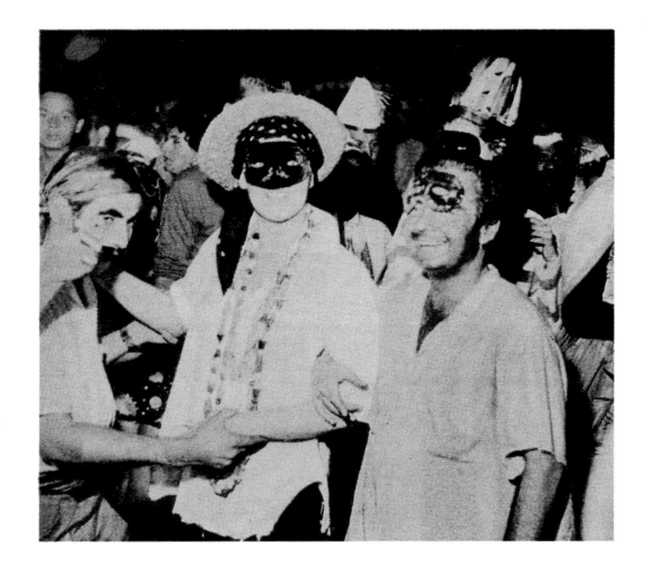

ly torn to make her look like a beggar. As a disguise for Jorginho, Kim improvised a moustache made of fur snipped from Zsa Zsa's Chihuahua. Kim's relationship with Zsa Zsa, never very cordial, only worsened after this unauthorized clipping. Zsa Zsa Gabor regretted having to leave her dog at Jorginho's home, but there was no alternative. The Copa's no-pets policy extended, that same year, to Joan Crawford (by then a significant shareholder and executive at Pepsi-Cola), who was not permitted to keep her two poodles in the hotel, and was forced to spend the night with them in her cabin on the transatlantic liner that had brought her to the country. The hotel had historic and good reasons for imposing these restrictions on its guests. Temporary home to millionaires and monarchs, the Copacabana Palace in 1942 became the permanent residence of King Carol II of Rumania, dethroned two years previously. Fleeing from political and family pressures, Carol arrived in Brazil with a retinue that included Magda Lupescu (the lover he was to marry in 1947) and the eight Pekinese dogs from which she was never separated. After eight years of residence, the little pack of dogs had ruthlessly destroyed the costly upholstery and curtains in the suite occupied by the couple. The damage was duly paid for, but it led Otávio Guinle to henceforth refuse guests with animals. In 1961, a professor named Jânio Quadros took over the presidency for a mere eight months. At the end of this period he resigned, compelled by "occult forces" that he never satisfactorily identified. His short government was characterized by histrionic acts, such as an attempt to prohibit two-piece bathing costumes, which he considered immoral. Naturally, these "daring" costumes had the sands of Copacabana as their greatest display window, and the residents of this neighbourhood (by now almost 200 thousand strong and unaccustomed to arbitrary repression) took no notice of the order from Brasília. Carnival of 1962 saw Rita Hayworth take Copacabana by storm. At 43, with five marriages and some fifty films under her belt, she arrived in Rio still exuding the beauty that made her one of the most sensual actresses of all time.

Kim Novak and Jorginho Guinle disguised as beggars (top), joined the crowds dancing in the streets

"I've come to see my friend Jorginho Guinle," she announced on her arrival at the Copa, from whence she was to conduct her feverish social schedule. The "eternal Gilda," wishing to see "the roots of carnival," went to Madureira (a suburb unknown to most foreigners) to watch a rehearsal of the Portela samba school. There she was bestowed the honour of parading as the school's standard bearer. Encouraged, the actress ordered a "Bahiana" costume and wore it to the Copa ball. Agreeing with her ex-husband Orson Welles, she went on to gush to the press: "He was right when he described the wonders I would experience in this country."

Rita Hayworth, the eternal Gilda, was the sensation of the 1962 carnival at the Copacabana Palace

BB AND THE PRICE OF LIBERTY

In 1963 it was Kirk Douglas's turn to experience carnival his way. In order to creatively, yet economically, promote the Brazilian launch of his film *Spartacus*, he turned up at all the balls wearing the same gladiator costume he wore in the film, thereby garnering widespread free publicity for the launch. But the real war was faced by Brigitte Bardot the following year. In January 1964 she landed in Rio in the company of Bob Zaguri, a young Moroccan playboy who lived in Copacabana and was, at that point, relatively unknown. At Rio airport, BB refused to get off the plane until the crowd of reporters awaiting her dispersed. As they refused to budge, she alighted shielding her face with her jacket and immediately raced off, leaving her mountains of baggage behind. This gesture seems to have egged the press on in their pursuit of her, and over the next few days the French actress remained besieged in her boyfriend's apartment, two blocks from the Copacabana Palace, under the implacable vigilance of dozens of telephoto lenses. Traffic in the environs became impossible, and Zaguri's neighbours threatened to expel him from the building. Finally, BB sent a message to the reporters: if they continued to stalk her and invade her privacy, she would cancel the three-month vacation she had planned in Brazil and return to Paris. This threat had no effect whatsoever, and the impasse was only breached with the intervention of public relations man Oscar Ornstein. In exchange for a complete halt of the siege upon the

K

Kirk Douglas (opposite, below) donned the costume from his latest film, "Spartacus", for the 1963 Copa ball. After heavy persecution by reporters, Brigitte Bardot (left, opposite and overleaf, above) called a truce, on the Copa terrace, 1964

During Rio's fourth centenary celebrations, the Copa put on the greatest of all its balls, "Old Rio." The high point was the costume competition, whose jury was presided by Romy Schneider (above, with Jorginho Guinle)

actress he proposed a press conference at the Copacabana Palace. All parties agreed, and over one hundred reporters signed up for the interview. BB arrived under heavy security, replied dryly to the questions, reluctantly agreed to a photo session on the verandah facing the beach, and closed the ordeal with a warning: "Let it be understood that as of right now you will stop persecuting me and leave me in peace." The dictate was honoured, and BB was able to travel to the still unexplored region of Búzios, a resort two hours away that the actress fell in love with and, through her presence, promoted internationally. While she was still on holiday, Brazil suffered a crisis with the removal of President João Goulart from office by a military coup that set in motion twenty years of dictatorship. None of this (neither the press nor the politics) soured Brigitte Bardot's memories of Brazil. Indeed, in 1965 she did not hesitate to return to Rio as the official guest of the municipal government to celebrate the fourth centenary of Rio's founding. During these celebrations the Copacabana Palace promoted its largest carnival ball ever, on the theme "Old Rio." Seven halls (five more than usual) were decorated to represent the landscape of the old streets of the city. The highlight of the evening, enlivened by 180 musicians and several orchestras, was the costume competition. (Among the jury members was Romy Schneider, best known in those days for her interpretation of Sissi, Empress of Austria.) In October, also part of the celebrations, the International Cinema Festival was staged. Held in prestige by delegations from around the world, it transformed the Copa's swimming pool into a tropical replica of the Croisette, featuring a constant parade of directors, critics and stars. Just as in Cannes, beautiful unknown girls exhibited their breasts along the beach in front of the hotel, hoping for the flash of glory, but, unlike in Cannes, this nudity attracted the attention of the police faster than that of any photographer. The festival also had the merit of bringing together, for the first time, young Brazilian screen actors and some of the myths of modern European cinema. Fritz Lang, director of *Metropolis* and *M*, and the greatest representative of German impressionist cinema, described *Vidas Secas* [Dry Lives], by Nelson Pereira dos Santos, and *Black God White Devil*, by Glauber Rocha, as "vigorous and revealing examples of the creative capacity of this country's directors." The quest for a mode of expression which departed from the norms dictated by Hollywood was central to the New Cinema movement in Brazil. This issue engaged all the festival participants in lively debates: Pole Jerzy Kawalerowicz *(Mother Joan of the Angels)* incited jealousy when he declared the Italy of Antonioni and Fellini to be at the forefront of this quest. To honour all the foreign delegations, the Copa decided to hold a Celebrities Ball. Italian actress Claudia Cardinale, then filming *Una rosa per tutti* [*A Rose for Everyone*], based on the play by Brazilian Gláucio Gil, disappointed her fans by claiming a sudden indisposition and failing to attend the ball. The event nevertheless hosted Warren Beatty, Mel Ferrer, Vincente Minnelli, Rossanna Podestà, Antonella Lualdi, Raf Vallone, Mitzi Gaynor, Lino Ventura and Dino de Laurentiis.

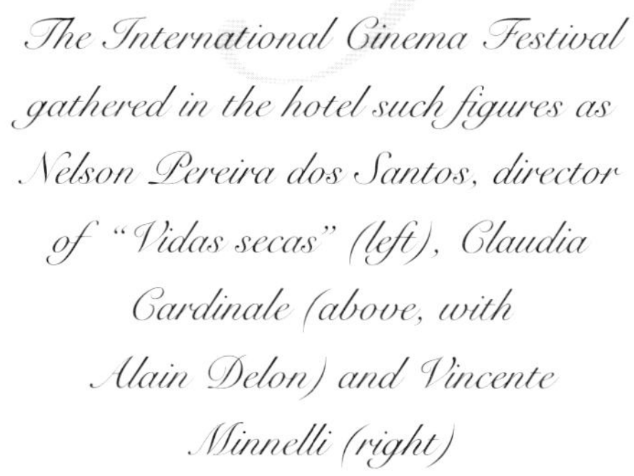

The International Cinema Festival gathered in the hotel such figures as Nelson Pereira dos Santos, director of "Vidas secas" (left), Claudia Cardinale (above, with Alain Delon) and Vincente Minnelli (right)

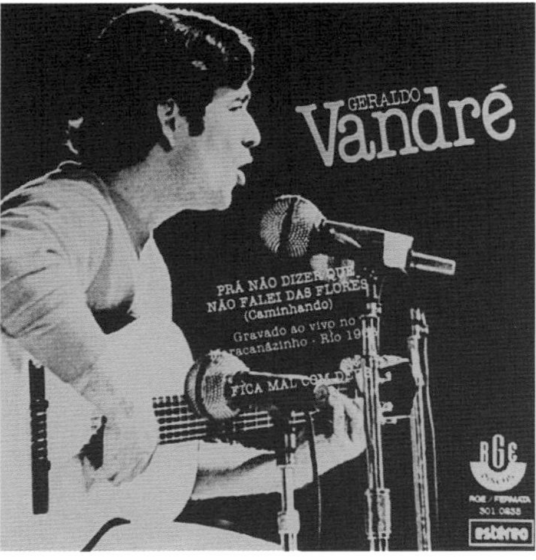

Glimpses of the song festival era: Nara Leão (top, left) and Geraldo Vandré (above). Gina Lollobrigida (top, with Dercy Gonçalves) enlivened the 1967 carnival

We want to be Gina!

Before 1965 was over the Copa would receive two royal couples: Baudouin and Fabiola of Belgium, and Rezah Pahlevi and Farah Diba of Iran. The European royal couple's visit was quick and uneventful, but the same cannot be said of the Shah's stay. The Brazilian Government, aware of its country's great dependence on Iranian oil, appealed to the hotel to grant lodging to the Empress's little dog, an exception that Otávio Guinle permitted on the condition that the animal be confined to a cage in the presidential suite. Pahlevi in turn requested a refrigerator stocked daily with Pepsi-Cola, which had not yet been launched in Rio. This caprice was satisfied by sending for a few cases of the beverage from Brazilian cities where it was undergoing market tests. The white caviar offered by Pahlevi for his banquet at the Copacabana Palace also caused logistical problems, this time with diplomatic consequences. The allotment of caviar shipped from Teheran was insufficient, with the result that the quota of caviar reserved for Buenos Aires, the next leg of the trip, was wolfed entirely by the two thousand *carioca* guests. This error in calculation cost the Iranian ambassador in Brasília his assignment, and within weeks he was banished to a post in Africa. In 1966, the First International Song Festival, destined to leave its mark on Brazilian cultural life, chose the Copacabana Palace for its administrative headquarters. A pioneer of large-scale musical performances, the Festival attracted 20 thousand spectators per night in the Maracanãzinho gymnasium – the largest crowd in the world yet gathered for a show of that type. Its organizer, journalist Augusto Marzagão, pulled off the feat of bringing dozens of influential foreign musicians to Rio to perform without pay. He seduced participants with free airfares and accommodation at the Copa, touting the festival as a "historic opportunity" to sing live to thousands of youths subjugated by a military dictatorship. "Getting to know Brazil's emerging market of music consumers was the initial motivation for many," recalls Marzagão, "but the appeal of joining a political cause was often the decisive factor." Until its demise in 1972, the Festival provided rare moments of collective liberty and would project a new generation of talent in Brazilian popular music; this was especially true of its competitive national stages, with up to four thousand entries in competition. The massive presence of journalists and foreign artists (forty countries participated in the Festival in just one year) helped to inhibit the censorious impetus of the Government, but could not entirely quash it. The most strained of the confrontations between the forces of political repression and the Festival occurred in 1967, when the Army took offense to a song by Geraldo Vandré, *Para não dizer que não falei de flores* [So You Won't Say I Never Spoke of Flowers]. While the composer hid from the police in a room at the Copa, Marzagão attempted to convince the generals that the image of the country was at risk, as the famous guests of the Festival were threatening not to perform out of sympathy for their persecuted Brazilian colleague. This threat had not actually been made, and probably could not have been organized in time, but the bluff worked. Temporarily reprieved, Vandré was able to stay in the competition, winning the sympathy of the audience and the third-place prize in the national phase. His joy, however, was short-lived. Weeks after the festival had ended and the audience dispersed, the composer was thrown in jail and his song banned. The foreign musicians' support of Geraldo Vandré was not the only gesture of solidarity to mark 1967. Invited by the Copacabana Palace to spend carnival in Rio that year, Gina Lollobrigida did not wish to limit herself to the oh-so-well-behaved programme prepared by the hotel. Instead, she decided to attend the "Baile dos Enxutos," promoted by homosexuals in the downtown São José the-

A group of singers staying at the Copa (above) during the First International Song Festival; Milton Nascimento (top, right), 1966

atre, and considered by the authorities unseemly for tourists. The unexpected appearance of the Italian star was greeted with delirious joy by hundreds of gays from Rio and other states, who heralded their new Muse with cries of "We want to be Gina!"

Gina Lollobrigida was elected the muse of Rio's gay community after her surprise appearance at the Gay Ball

OTÁVIO'S LEGACY

The following year, 1968, was marked by increasing student unrest, to which the military government responded by decreeing Institutional Act No. 5, the most truculent in a series of despotic measures. It was also the year the Copacabana Palace lost its founder. On the night of May 14, Otávio Guinle succumbed, at 81, to pulmonary emphysema in the presidential suite where he lived. His death generated speculation about the future of the hotel. His widow, Maria Isabel de Lafayette Rodrigues Pereira Guinle, with whom he had maintained a relationship since the mid-1940's (they were formally married on January 10, 1957), had no management experience, and the couple's two children were still too young to fill their father's shoes. In spite of the obvious difficulties, Dona Mariazinha (as she was known) assumed the job, determined to rise to the challenge and conquer the spectre of bankruptcy without compromising the Copa's mystique. She was to remain firmly at the helm for the next 21 years. Paradoxically, she soon realized that for her mission to succeed it would be necessary to bury all vestiges of her husband's managerial romanticism, which had ignored, with a dreamer's disdain, the basic cost/benefit ratios of hotel management. Otávio had never permitted any cutting of corners, and now losses were piling up, balance sheet after balance sheet. The Copacabana Palace had the highest guest/staff ratio in the world, and indulged in absurd luxuries, maintaining services on-site that

With the death of Otávio Guinle (above) in 1968, Dona Mariazinha undertook the difficult task of succeeding her husband; a portrait (top) of José Eduardo Guinle, the couple's son, by Boris Smirnoff

The barber shop (top) and the pressing and starching department of the Glória Laundry (above)

could only have been justified in the days when the hotel was miles away from the closest shops. As a result of this philosophy, the hotel maintained in operation an aviary, a butcher, a carpentry, a workshop for the restoration of ornaments, an elevator repair shop, a barber shop, a print shop, curtain-makers, upholsterers, and countless other services and specialized employees, with all their resultant costs, all of which had long been contracted out by modern hoteliers. Otávio Guinle had also established a generous relationship with his more than 1400 permanent employees, distributing 10% of the gross profits of the hotel to them. In direct contradiction to this philosophy, Dona Mariazinha had, within a few months, halved the operation her husband had left her. Although she faced hefty severance payments and complaints from guests and old friends, her strategy saved the Copacabana Palace from financial ruin, allowing it to once again become profitable. This recovery enabled the hotel, beginning in the 1970's, to face challenges unheard of in its history. Attracted by the Government's fiscal incentives, big international chains began building a series of modern hotels in the South Zone, dramatically increasing the competition in the field. The inherent characteristics of an old building, such as the lack of central air-conditioning, were just part of the problem that reduced the competitiveness of the fifty-year-old Copacabana Palace. Typical of the beginning of the century, the hotel was a monument to luxury designed for guests who would spend long periods there with their families. Finding ways of adjusting to the new market profile, characterized by busy jet-age executives, became the Copacabana Palace's basic objective, which Mariazinha Guinle summed up with the phrase "to modernize without vulgarizing." The principal aim was to maintain the hotel as a matchless reference of sophistication and good taste in South America, and not just for the exclusive enjoyment of the guests. In November of 1968, for example, the Copacabana Palace was invited to prepare the dinner hosted by Queen Elizabeth II and Prince Phillip in Rio, the most important social event in the country that year. Since only the hotel owned a *vermeil* service for two hundred, sufficient to attend to the number of guests, the 19th-century dinner service and cutlery left the confines of the Copa for the first time, under strong security escort, and travelled to the São Clemente Palace, residence of the British ambassador and venue of the banquet.

1969 also saw many illustrious guests come and go. The list included, among others, Indira Ghandi, Wernher von Braun, Princess Margrethe of Denmark and Princes Akihito and Michiko of Japan. However, an incident that will forever be associated with that era in the hotel's history involved Nelson Rockefeller, then Governor of New York. During his visit to Latin America as President Nixon's emissary, he chose the Modern Art Museum of Rio, which he already favoured with personal contributions, as the location for a press conference on his mission in Brazil. A fortunate coincidence prevented the meeting from resulting in a political crime which would have had tragic international repercussions. While making a phone call at the Copacabana Palace, where Rockefeller was a guest, general manager Dario Vasconcellos Campos happened to intercept a crossed line and heard two unidentifiable speakers mentioning the words "bomb" and "museum." The conversation was immediately reported to the police, who submitted the Museum to a thorough sweep; Rockefeller delayed his arrival at the museum under the pretext of receiving a group of university students at the Copa for a private discussion. During this encounter with the mythical students, the search of the museum turned up an explosive device, but official censorship impeded the news from reaching the newspapers. The episode resulted in a personal letter from Rockefeller, which, without directly mentioning the incident, thanked manager Dario Campos for his assistance. Continuing in its race towards modernization, in 1970 the Copacabana Palace began the first overall restoration of its facilities since the construction of the Annexe. The work was essential to reduce the hotel's disadvantages in relation to the competition waiting to be inaugurated, as it was unable to confront this competition merely on the strength of its history, charm and tradition. Nevertheless, these intangible qualities continued to attract guests from all over the world, even those who did not particularly appreciate them. Possibly this seductiveness explains the sudden appearance of Janis Joplin at the Copacabana Palace in February 1970, eight months before her death in Hollywood from a heroin overdose. Janis abandoned the anonymity in which she had been living for nearly a month, during which she circulated around Rio as a simple tourist, and moved to the Copa to spend her last few days in the city. Excepting an interview with reporters

Two illustrious visitors during 1969 – Nelson Rockefeller (top) and Princess Margrethe of Denmark (below)

specializing in pop music and a few poolside photos, no other record remains of the singer's stay at the hotel. Staff who attended her recall a seemingly fragile hippie with a permanent thirst for vodka. The artist herself, however, harboured stronger memories of the time, as revealed by her sister, Laura, in her book *Love, Janis*. In a letter published therein, the most influential representative of the Woodstock generation confessed that she had found the great love of her life, who remained unidentified, in Brazil. "He really loved me," she wrote, "I thought I would die, all alone except for the fans who followed me everywhere. But he was real and, who knows, maybe I'll get tired of the music industry. But right now I'm really involved in it." As of the early days of the 1970's, visits to Brazil by Hollywood stars became increasingly rare. While this void was partially filled by European stars (who cultivated cultural ties with the Brazilian New Cinema movement), Rio was never again to receive groups as large as those organized by Jorginho Guinle. Those kinds of tours, in which the participants were rewarded with no more than sunshine and fun, were squeezed out of the stars' increasingly professional agendas. Their visits began to focus less on their personal wishes and more on studio marketing dictates. Other genres, such as pop music, dance, fashion and sports, diluted the enthusiasm the masses had previously devoted almost exclusively to the cinema. This phenomenon was compounded by the advent of television and video, which took the stars into the homes of their fans. Spotting them in the flesh at the entrance to a hotel or a gala ball just wasn't as much fun as it used to be. Nevertheless, the Copacabana Palace continued to fill its Golden Book with collectible autographs during this scarcity of Hollywood representatives. Rudolf Nureyev, avidly admired by many Brazilians, was received at the Copacabana Palace in 1971 and lavished with special attentions. The care that surrounded his stay even involved décor changes to his room, placing the head of his bed in the direction of the

A hippie at the Pérgola, Janis Joplin (above); dancer Rudolf Nureyev (right)

sunrise, in accordance with the dancer's request. However, the sun's influence was not particularly positive. During his opening night, Nureyev snatched the baton out of Brazilian maestro Isaac Karabtchevsky's hand and, to the bafflement of the Municipal Theatre orchestra, began with nervous gestures to indicate the desired musical tempo. Despite this disaster, it was decided to maintain the bed permanently in the position determined by the illustrious guest. In that year Copacabana was home to 240 thousand inhabitants and still growing. The privileged location of the Copacabana Palace – facing the sea, at the heart of the neighbourhood – led to several attempts to buy it, all manner of development being envisaged for its more than 12 thousand square yards. Offers varied widely, but always involved sums far more attractive than the hotel's turnover, limited as it was by its small number of rooms and dropping room rates. All of the proposed projects, however, evaporated in the face of Dona Mariazinha's conviction not to allow the palace inaugurated by her husband in 1923 to disappear. So it was that in 1973 Luiz Eduardo and José Eduardo Guinle, Dona Mariazinha's two sons and chief executives, commissioned architect Theor Loher to design three commercial buildings (the largest was to be 32 storeys tall) on the Copa's land – carefully keeping their mother out of the early stages of the plan. The initiative, quickly approved by local urban planning agencies, brought into the open a widespread discussion on the demolition of the hotel; it divided the opinions of politicians, historians, journalists and the populace in general. The debate took on enormous proportions, and President Geisel reacted by ordering the governor of Rio, Chagas Freitas, to find a means of "avoiding the disappearance of a hotel to which an authentic historical value can be attributed." Chagas immediately charged the National Historic Patrimony Service with evaluating whether the Copacabana Palace could be registered as a Heritage Site. Faced with this possibility, eldest brother Luiz Eduardo protested against official intervention in the family's affairs, admitting publicly for the first time that the hotel, born of his father's dream sixty years previously, had become an "irrecuperable liability," to the point of forcing the cancellation of such traditional and successful events as the carnival ball. At the height of the

Despite the hotel's financial difficulties, the celebrities kept on coming, among them actress Natalie Wood, snapped in a carefree moment at the 1968 Copa ball

Rod Stewart, expelled from the hotel for hosting a football match in his suite

polemic, in 1974, an episode occurred that did not reach the newspapers but that symbolically seemed to deal the first blow of the wrecking ball to the Copacabana Palace. The incident was the work of Alice Cooper, one of the biggest names in hard rock at the time. Back at the hotel after performing at Maracanãzinho gymnasium, Cooper, his band and his technical team staged an even more explosive "show" than the one that had induced such delirium in their fans. During the wee hours, deaf to the appeals from management and the protests of other guests, the group razed their hotel rooms, hurling plates and food around and tossing objects from the windows in a monumental drunken rampage. The result of all this fun was four demolished suites, damaged furniture, broken windows; the hotel swimming pool was empty for the two days required for the removal of the bottles, cutlery, glasses and other items thrown there by Cooper and his companions. For some time there was concern about the whereabouts of a large python that accompanied the rock star on his tours, obliging the hotel security to institute a careful search of the hotel premises. Fortunately for all concerned, the elusive reptile had not come to Rio. Restitution for all the damage caused by Alice Cooper was made with the payment of the largest bill for extras ever registered by the hotel cashier. For years the authorities neither prohibited nor permitted the demolition of the Copacabana Palace, placing the Guinle family in an increasingly uncomfortable position with successive governments. This lack of definition prevented essential improvements from being made to the hotel, since the owners were unable to plan for the future. All that remained was to face reality, but never at the expense of old principles. This attitude became clear when, in 1977, rock star Rod Stewart and his musicians were expelled from the Copacabana Palace by order of Luiz Eduardo Guinle after playing a noisy game of football in the ample, but for these purposes inadequate, presidential suite. The game provoked complaints from neighbouring guests, broke a picture, and soiled several walls. Eight years later, invited to sing at the Rock in Rio Festival, the English star showed he harboured no ill feelings by requesting a reservation at the Copa. The request, however, was turned down due to "lack of vacancies." In 1980, the Guinles commissioned a new design from architect Paulo Casé, more daring than that of Theor Loher, to replace the Copacabana Palace with a complex of five buildings, the tallest over 40 storeys high. They would house two hotels, offices, shops, a cultural outlet with theatres and cinemas, six restaurants and a leisure area open to the public. Defending his clients, Casé affirmed that "hotels in the style of the Copacabana Palace have lost their competitiveness to others better adapted to today's tourism, with a larger number of rooms in far smaller spaces." Once again *cariocas* took up the defense of the hotel in spite of the losses the proprietors were sustaining. To settle the issue, the Federal Cultural Council even proposed a referendum, while a petition with 20 thousand signatures requested the judicial protection of the property. In 1982, Governor Leonel Brizola tried to reconcile both factions and suggested that the Casé design be modified so as to preserve the hotel's main building, as an emblem of Rio. In exchange Brizola would allow the Annexe, the old Casino, the Golden Room and the theatre to be demolished to make room for the new buildings. The compromise was accepted – but even so it was not successful. The following year, under public pressure, the very same Brizola approved the registration of the Copacabana Palace as a national treasure, in an act endorsed six months later by the National Historical and Artistic Heritage Secretariat. The hotel's worsening financial picture, however, was defeating Mariazinha Guinle's last and best efforts. Much to the surprise of the press and many of her friends, she referred to the official enshrinement of the hotel as a "back-handed gift," stating that the Copacabana Palace was no more than "a nice building, with no historical value." This attitude was pure bravado, as time would soon prove. If on the one hand economic factors led Mariazinha Guinle to issue such statements, on the other hand she held fast to the traditions of the Copacabana Palace and the routines she held so dear. Such was the case when she refused to accommodate King Juan Carlos and Queen Sofia in 1982. As a security measure, the Spanish embassy requested that the sixth floor of the hotel be completely blocked off, which meant that Otávio Guinle's widow would have to vacate the suite she had been living in since 1953. To the embarrassment of the Brazilian Government and the astonishment of the competition, the demands

"I had the good fortune of knowing the Copacabana Palace in 1928 ... I admire it, and I performed here, and this is one of my fondest memories ..."
Jean Sablon

were considered "unacceptable" and the royal reservations were cancelled, in what was probably a unique happening in the world of hotel management. Even during those precarious years at the Copacabana Palace, the thick pages of its Golden Book, yellowed with time, collected affectionate messages from those who had lived unforgettable moments at the hotel. One such message was from French singer Jean Sablon, in 1984, during one of many stops on his worldwide farewell tour. Between the signatures of President João Figueiredo and American actor Richard Gere, Sablon wrote: "I had the good fortune of knowing the Copacabana Palace in 1928 ... I admire it, and I performed here, and this is one of my fondest memories ..." There was no lack of memories at a special dinner in a private salon of the Copacabana Palace in 1986; General Vernon Walters dined with Brazilian officers alongside whom he had fought during the Second World War. Former vice-director of the CIA and the U.S. ambassador to the United Nations, Walters spent the night reliving war stories with his old comrades, unaware that he would be under attack once again the very next day. Upon leaving an interview at the Hotel Glória, he was showered with eggs thrown by a group of students brandishing posters accusing him of collaborating with the recently terminated military dictatorship. Walters escaped unscathed from the ambush, and commented on the enemy's aim: "Disappointing," he said dryly. "The mob was very small and the eggs not even rotten ..."

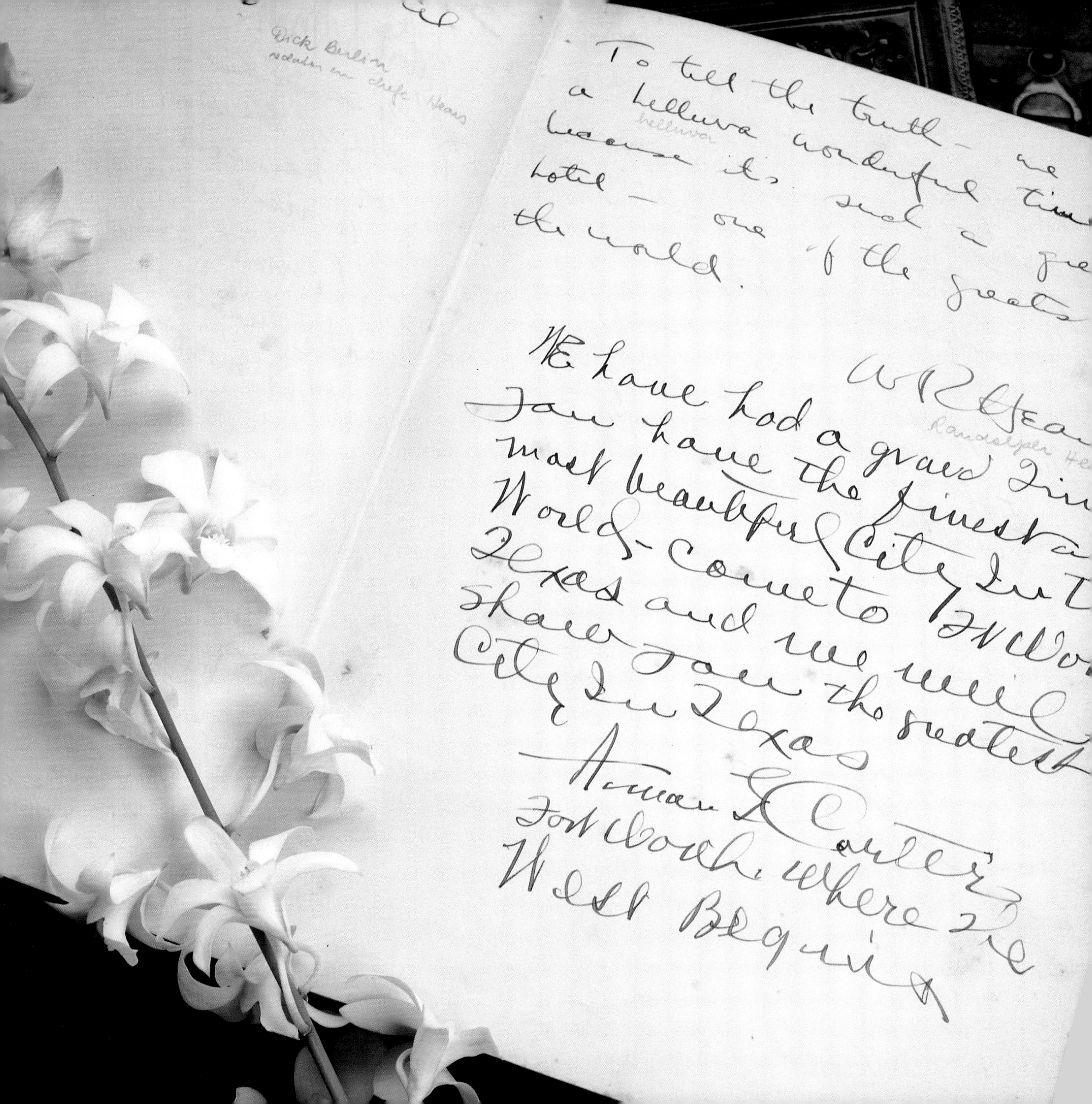

Dick Berlin
redator em chefe Hearst

To tell the truth – we
a helluva wonderful time
helluva
because it's such a gre
hotel – one of the greatest
the world.

W R Hear
Randolph Hea

We have had a grand tim
You have the finest a
most beautiful City in t
World – come to the Wor
Texas and we will
show you the greatest
City in Texas

Amon G. Carter
Fort Worth, Where the
West Begins

CHAPTER SIX

The Jewel of the Collection

From the Guinles to Sherwood

The Guinles, increasingly harried by the competition, continued on their quest for a solution to the hotel's problems. The press had picked up on the drop in standards, although the loyal clientele could still look on the bright side. "Old, decadent, but dignified ... Just how I like it," announced writer Gore Vidal in 1987 as he entered his suite. "I am the third generation of my family to stay here," recalled the author, who was in Brazil for the launch of his book of essays *Matters of Fact and of Fiction*. The absence of funds for the upkeep of the hotel, and the awful possibility of watching it turn into an "archeological ruin" – in the words of Luiz Eduardo Guinle – galvanized the hotel's important allies. In the closing scenes of that over-long soap opera, the Municipal Chamber of Rio, in a session that witnessed actual fistfights among its aldermen, approved the "partial protection" of the Copacabana Palace; this would allow the construction of two 27-storey buildings, to be designed by Edson Musa, at the rear of the main building. The ultimate irony of all this was that no investors could be found for the ambitious project. 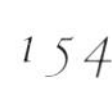 On the one hand, this situation relieved the conservationists; on the other, it kept the Copacabana Palace inexorably on the path to bankruptcy – which outcome was only avoided by a quirk of fate. American businessman James Blair Sherwood, Kentucky-born and resident in Great Britain, had been coming

to Rio for several years, as his company, Sea Containers, had interests here. His determination to build up an international network of tourism enterprises of unsurpassed tradition and elegance was fortified by the acquisition, in 1976, of the classic Hotel Cipriani in Venice. When, six years later, he bought the Orient Express, the romantic railway immortalized by Agatha Christie in her famous detective story, he attracted the world's attention. Sherwood had stayed at the Copacabana Palace on several occasions and admired it; now he resolved to turn it into the first Southern Hemisphere jewel in his collection. His resolve strengthened when he discovered that the original turn-of-the-century architectural design by Joseph Gire contained some entirely unique features, which it would be impossible to reproduce today. It would, however, take three years of slow negotiations before the deal could be concluded. Mariazinha Guinle herself was partly responsible for the delay: for months, she kept secret the letter in which Sherwood proposed they open negotiations. Silently, Otávio Guinle's widow had returned to her former conviction of keeping her husband's hotel in the family. Quite by accident, the buried proposal became public – Luiz Eduardo Guinle happened to bump into one of Sherwood's emissaries, who demanded a progress report on the situation – and Dona Mariazinha at last relented, this time for good, to the pressure of her sons and the advice of two long-time friends, lawyer José Bulhões Pedreira and banker Walter Moreira Salles. Finally in 1989 the widow sold the controlling interest in the Copacabana Palace to the owner of Sea Containers. The sale was hugely newsworthy, and not just because it involved the most famous hotel in Brazil. As it happened, it coincided with the first presidential election by direct vote since the imposition of the military regime 25 years previously. At the time of the sale, a bitter dispute was raging between candidates Lula and Collor – their platforms on the question of foreign capital and investment in the country could not have been more divergent. When the contract with the Guinles was signed, Lula was leading the polls, which further fuelled the fears of foreign investors in Brazil. The owner of Sea Containers was undeterred, however, and in spite of the advice of his auditors, he not only acquired the hotel for 23 million dollars, but also initiated the largest-scale restoration ever undertaken on the building, at a cost of almost double the sale price. Under the supervision of decorator Gerard Gallet, in

Following lengthy negotiations, the Copacabana Palace was sold to businessman James Sherwood in 1989

The new management undertook extensive restoration of the Copa, supervised by decorator Gerard Gallet

charge of other restorations within the Orient Express Hotels group, the refurbishment affected the very structure of the building, damaged by time and badly carried-out restorations in the past. The façade of the Copacabana Palace was entirely rejuvenated, and an ingenious lighting system restored its special glow to the nocturnal landscape of Copacabana beach. Within the hotel, the Bife de Ouro was replaced by a Rio branch of Venice's Cipriani restaurant, under the management of Italian chef Francesco Carli. 1996 confirmed the wisdom of this particular innovation when Rio's Cipriani was voted one of the ten best hotel restaurants in the world by the American magazine *Hotels*. It was only after the death of Dona Mariazinha Guinle, in April 1993, that Sherwood approved alterations to the sixth floor, where the former proprietress of the hotel had continued to live until her death. The two presidential suites were broken up into seven large suites with their own exclusive black-granite swimming pool. The fifth floor was also modified, implementing a business centre and executive suites. Remodelling of the remaining floors did not impinge on the original plan of the hotel, so modernization, fortunately, did not take place at the expense of the hotel's original features. The number of rooms and suites – including those in the Annexe – rose from 223 to 226, thereby preserving the former guest/space ratio. All private and public rooms were soundproofed. Reception and lobby facilities for the Annexe and the main building were centralized; bathers were given their own access, bypassing the lobby; a tennis court was built on the terrace adjacent to the rear of the hotel. The romanticism of the Pérgola was maintained, surrounded by white trellis work; in addition to its usual service, the habit of serving afternoon tea was revived. Every aspect of the work was executed with extreme caution, under the permanent supervision of the Ministry of Culture's Historical Heritage Department. Every step of the process was carried out with the utmost attention to detail. All the doors and windows were restored, and when this was not feasible, craftsmen re-made them as they would have in 1923; the same applied to mirrors, lighting fixtures and crystal. In the salons, pillars crafted of marble from played-out mines underwent the same exacting process; over one thousand square yards of fabric were produced exclusively for the hotel. Carpets, drapes and upholstery for the Golden Room were imported from France. Even during the restoration work,

The Bife de Ouro was replaced by Cipriani, a success headed by chef Francesco Carli

The Cipriani was rated by American magazine "Hotels" one of the ten best hotel restaurants in the world

A series of photos of Princess Diana at the Copa swimming pool became famous around the world

which called for alternately closing the main building or the Annexe, the Copacabana Palace continued to receive notable guests. In 1991, Nelson Mandela, accompanied by his wife Winnie, was received by the hotel as Head of State, despite the visit being well in advance of the elections that would make Mandela the first coloured President of South Africa. The couple occupied the presidential suite, but did not see their country's flag fluttering on the Avenida Atlântica façade: the Brazilian foreign office maintained friendly relations with the Pretoria regime. Mandela, who drew crowds wherever he went, arrived in Brazil with no more than the clothes on his back, as his retinue's baggage had been held up in Miami; a makeshift wardrobe was put together for him, hastily purchased by the hotel management. Notwithstanding the charisma of the leader of the African National Congress, 1991's most celebrated visitors were Prince Charles and Princess Diana; they came to Brazil to fulfill a busy official schedule, and stimulated huge interest among the press and the local population. In order give the couple the necessary privacy, the Copa's presidential suite was "walled" by a row of large potted shrubs, arranged along the verandah in front of their rooms so as to screen the interior of the apartment. All this was made necessary by relentless photographers of various nationalities who had rented windows in neighbouring buildings in their dogged determination to snap the Royal couple unawares. As it happened and despite all the precautions taken, photos of Princess Di taken in the Copacabana Palace received massive international media attention. They were taken on the second day of the visit, when she was unaware of being observed. Prince Charles had travelled to Amazonia for a meeting, while Princess Diana had remained in Rio, to attend a presentation of the Brazilian ballet troupe Grupo Corpo. After the performance, at two in the morning, she decided to leave her room for some exercise. At the Princess's request, the lights around the hotel's swimming pool were turned on, and she swam for half an hour, completely alone, wearing a discreet blue bathing costume. Her elegant demeanour, both in and out of the water, were recorded by a sleepless *paparazzo* who had set up a vigil in the neighbouring Chopin building. Almost every major paper and magazine in the world ran those rare images of the solitary Princess in her bathing costume. Another famous British subject made headlines a few months later during his stay at the

Copacabana Palace. Engaged to perform at Rock in Rio II, singer George Michael surprised the organizers of the music festival by submitting a 55-page list of requirements for his stay in the city. The artist's whims included the demand that his clothes and those of his musicians be washed exclusively in biodegradable soap; a ban on the use of plastic items in his apartment; custom menus for twenty of his fifty followers and a selection of at least thirteen dishes at breakfast. During this same trip George Michael met stylist Anselmo Feleppa, whose companion he became until the latter's death three years later and to whom he dedicated the song *I Want your Sex* and, later, the album *Older*.

The original design of the hotel was adhered to throughout the refurbishment

Return to the Good Old Days

Little by little and thanks to the improvements it underwent after being bought by James Sherwood, the Copacabana Palace recovered the ability to face the competition that had sprung up during the 1970's and '80's; during this time, major international and national hotel chains had inaugurated five-star hotels in Rio, three of them actually on Avenida Atlântica. Recognition that the Copa had returned to its former glory occurred in 1992, during the United Nations Conference on the Environment and Development, Eco-92. Twelve heads of state were guests of the hotel, which was also chosen as the venue for the banquet Chinese prime minister, Li Peng, offered to the communist leaders present at Eco-92, among whom was Fidel Castro. Already studded with the signatures of so many of the world's leaders, 1992's Golden Book contained a name which brought back happy memories to the Copa: Beatrice Welles Smith. Orson Welles's daughter had returned to the city where her father lived in 1942 for the launch of the restored *Othello*. A few weeks later, in 1993, Chuck Berry and Louis Malle both held eyebrow-raising press conferences at the hotel. The aging rock star shocked his fans by declaring that he had never produced music for any reason other than to make money, while the French film director sparked off heated debates in the

Twelve heads of state elected to make the Copacabana Palace their headquarters during Eco-92

During the 1990's, the parade of celebrities continues: Calvin Klein (above) and Franco Zefirelli (below)

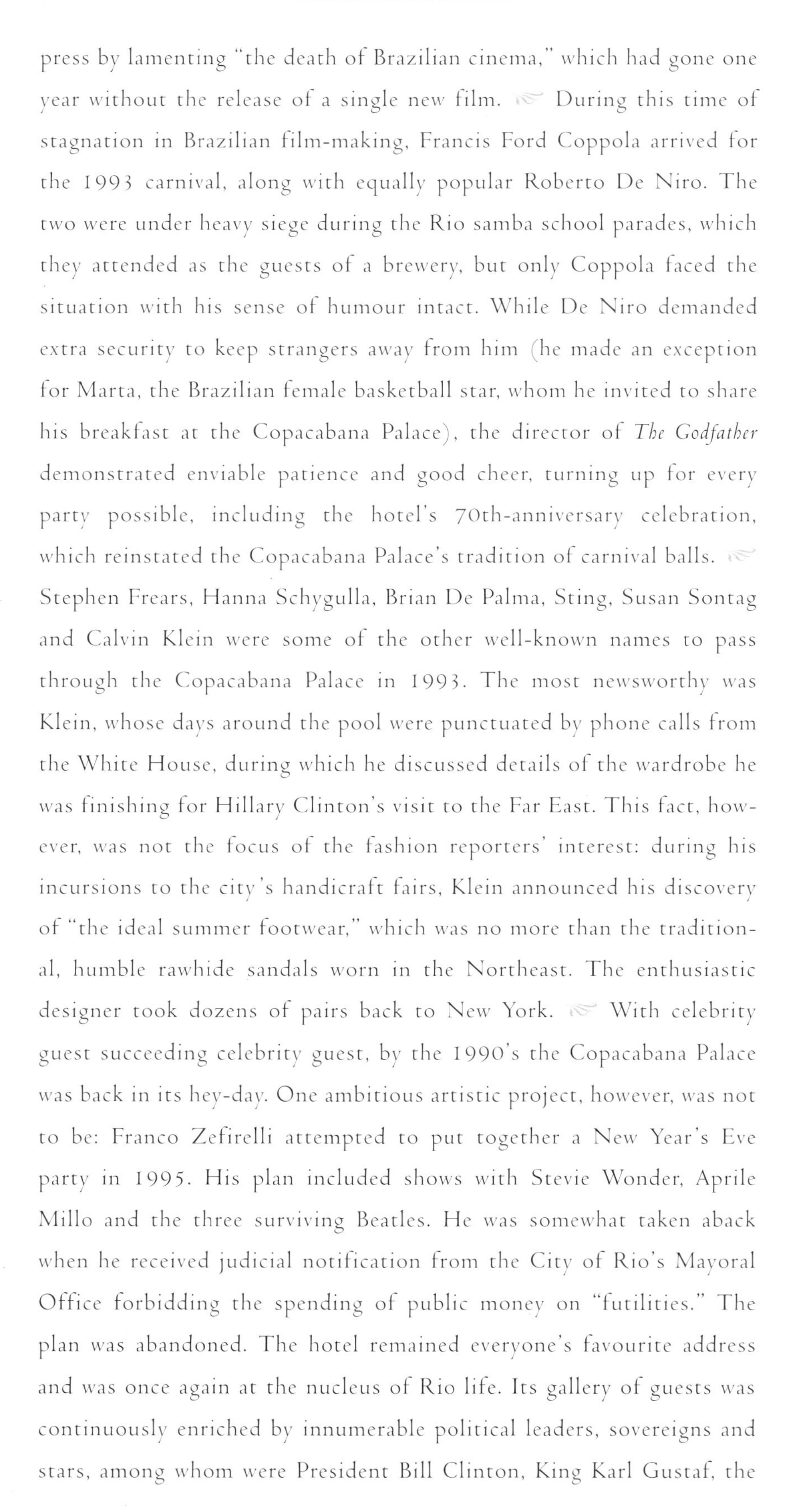

press by lamenting "the death of Brazilian cinema," which had gone one year without the release of a single new film. During this time of stagnation in Brazilian film-making, Francis Ford Coppola arrived for the 1993 carnival, along with equally popular Roberto De Niro. The two were under heavy siege during the Rio samba school parades, which they attended as the guests of a brewery, but only Coppola faced the situation with his sense of humour intact. While De Niro demanded extra security to keep strangers away from him (he made an exception for Marta, the Brazilian female basketball star, whom he invited to share his breakfast at the Copacabana Palace), the director of *The Godfather* demonstrated enviable patience and good cheer, turning up for every party possible, including the hotel's 70th-anniversary celebration, which reinstated the Copacabana Palace's tradition of carnival balls. Stephen Frears, Hanna Schygulla, Brian De Palma, Sting, Susan Sontag and Calvin Klein were some of the other well-known names to pass through the Copacabana Palace in 1993. The most newsworthy was Klein, whose days around the pool were punctuated by phone calls from the White House, during which he discussed details of the wardrobe he was finishing for Hillary Clinton's visit to the Far East. This fact, however, was not the focus of the fashion reporters' interest: during his incursions to the city's handicraft fairs, Klein announced his discovery of "the ideal summer footwear," which was no more than the traditional, humble rawhide sandals worn in the Northeast. The enthusiastic designer took dozens of pairs back to New York. With celebrity guest succeeding celebrity guest, by the 1990's the Copacabana Palace was back in its hey-day. One ambitious artistic project, however, was not to be: Franco Zefirelli attempted to put together a New Year's Eve party in 1995. His plan included shows with Stevie Wonder, Aprile Millo and the three surviving Beatles. He was somewhat taken aback when he received judicial notification from the City of Rio's Mayoral Office forbidding the spending of public money on "futilities." The plan was abandoned. The hotel remained everyone's favourite address and was once again at the nucleus of Rio life. Its gallery of guests was continuously enriched by innumerable political leaders, sovereigns and stars, among whom were President Bill Clinton, King Karl Gustaf, the

Rolling Stones and U2. A more recent visitor in this parade of the distinguished has been Peruvian writer Mario Vargas Llosa. He stayed at the hotel while taking part in the Brazilian Academy of Letters' centenary celebrations. On his departure, he wrote his farewell to the hotel in the Golden Book. His message sums up the feelings of the countless friends the Copacabana Palace has welcomed over a span of nearly eight decades: "I am happy to have spent a few days in this beautiful hotel in this beautiful city, which is, as this precious book attests, a piece of the history of our times. If these walls (ceilings, chairs, beds) could speak, what wondrous and terrible things they would say." Many of these

James Sherwood and his first Southern Hemisphere jewel

stories will never be told. They are lost in time, gone with those who took part in them or hidden behind the silence of those who witnessed them. Solidly built facing a sea that has challenged it since the beginning of the century, the Copacabana Palace has written its history with dreams. Dreams peopled by stars, kings and queens, myths and gods of our era, whose memories waft through the halls ("walls, ceilings, chairs, beds") like guests captive in the palace where they were born. This soul, bestowed only by time, is the Copacabana Palace's greatest asset. Nothing new can have these charms and mysteries. James Sherwood has no intention of placing this mystic soul at risk when he and his executives study plans for the future of the Copacabana Palace. Philip Carruthers, whom Sherwood nominated managing director as soon as he bought the hotel from the Guinle family, thinks no differently. "The projects we analyse are merely small operating adjustments, to incorporate into our daily life what technology and advances in hotel management have to offer. But we are fully aware of the richness of our past – and we know it to be our greatest asset. The future of the Copacabana Palace is not open to debate; it was defined in 1923 when Otávio Guinle opened the doors of the monument he had envisaged."

Robert De Niro (above, left), Brian De Palma (above, right) and Francis Ford Coppola (below) stayed at the Copa in 1993

COPACABA
E

A PALACE
NATAN
TAXI

Thanks

The author wish to thank the following people, whose contributions in the form of time, patience, memories and mementoes have been indispensible to the preparation of this book:

Adirson de Barros, Anna Maria Cavalcanti Bahiana, Antônio Pereira dos Santos, Augusto Marzagão, Carlos Niemeyer, Carmélia Alves, Claudia Fialho, Dario Vasconcellos Campos, Eliana Pittman, Eugenio Lyra Filho (in memoriam), Fernanda Montenegro, Fernando Aguinaga, Fernando Carlos de Andrade, Fernando Newlands, Fred Sill, General Aurélio F. Guimarães, Gilda Muller, Glorinha Drummond Sued, Hans Stern, Haroldo Costa, Harry Stone, Iberê Magnani, Iliana Cooper, Ivo Pitanguy, Jean Boghicci, Joaquim Monteiro de Carvalho, Jorge Guinle, Letícia and Murilo Neri, Luiz Eduardo Guinle, Lygia and Marcelo Lobo Machado, Manuel Bernardez Müller, Marina Isabel de Almeida Neves, Mario Gibson Barboza, Mario Pacheco, Mário Priolli, Mariozinho de Oliveira, Miriam Atalla, Nancy Winters, Nélson Tolipan, Octávio Guinle Filho, Osias Wurman, Oswaldo Miranda, Paulo Fernando Marcondes Ferraz, Philip Carruthers, Pomona Politis, Ricardo Amaral, Ricardo Cravo Albin, Roberto Medina, Rubens H. Riet, Sandra Bernhardt, Sérgio Augusto, Sérgio Cabral, Tatiana Leskova, Teophilo de Azeredo Santos and William Walter Pretyman.

Selected Bibliography

General Reference Works

BARBOZA, Mário Gibson. *Na diplomacia, o traço todo da vida*. Rio de Janeiro, Editora Record, 1992.
BENCHIMOL, Jaime Larry. *Pereira Passos: um Haussman tropical*. Rio de Janeiro, Secretaria Municipal de Cultura, Turismo e Esportes, Departamento Geral de Documentação e Informática, 1992.
BERGER, Eneida and Paulo. *História dos subúrbios: Copacabana*. Distrito Federal, Departamento de História e Documentação da Prefeitura do DF, 1959.
CALDEIRA, Jorge. *Viagem pela história do Brasil*. São Paulo, Companhia das Letras, 1997.
COARACY, Vivaldo. *Memórias da cidade do Rio de Janeiro*. Belo Horizonte, São Paulo, Itatiaia, Edusp, 1988.
Copacabana 1892/1922 – Subsídios para a sua história. Rio de Janeiro, Empresa de Turismo do Município do Rio de Janeiro, 1992.
CRULS, Gastão. *Aparência do Rio de Janeiro*. Rio de Janeiro, José Olympio, 1965.
DEBRET, J. *Viagem pitoresca ao Brasil*. São Paulo, Martins, 1954.
DINES, Alberto. *Morte no paraíso: a tragédia de Stefan Zweig*. Rio de Janeiro, Editora Nova Fronteira, 1981.
EFEGÊ, Jota. *Figuras e coisas do carnaval carioca*. Rio de Janeiro, Funarte, 1982.
GOLD, Arthur and FIZDALE, Robert. *A divina Sarah*. São Paulo, Companhia das Letras, 1994.
GONZAGA, Alice. *50 anos de Cinédia*. Rio de Janeiro, Editora Record, 1987.
GUEIROS, José A. *A história de um príncipe*. Rio de Janeiro, Distribuidora Record de Serviços de Imprensa, 1977.
GUINLE, Jorge. *Um século de boa vida*. São Paulo, Editora Globo, 1997.
JOBIM, Helena. *Antônio Carlos Jobim, um homem iluminado*. Rio de Janeiro, Editora Nova Fronteira, 1996.
JOFFILY, José. *Londres e Londrina*. Rio de Janeiro, Editora Paz e Terra, 1985.
LEITE, Miriam Moreira. *A condição feminina no Rio de Janeiro no século XIX*. São Paulo, Hucitec, 1984.
NICÉIAS, Alcides. *Verbetes para um dicionário do carnaval brasileiro*. Sorocaba, Fundação Ubaldino do Amaral, 1991.
PEREIRA, Simone Andrade. Tese: *Os anos dourados: Copacabana e o imaginário urbano dos anos cinqüenta*. In: Revista Vozes, nº 5, agosto de 1997.
QUEIROZ, Maria Isaura Pereira. *Carnaval brasileiro: o vivido e o mito*. São Paulo, Editora Brasiliense, 1992.
RENAULT, Delso. *O dia-a-dia no Rio de Janeiro segundo os jornais*. Rio de Janeiro, Civilização Brasileira, 1982.
SAIA, Luiz Henrique. *Carmen Miranda*. São Paulo, Editora Brasiliense, 1984.
SANTOS, Joaquim Ferreira dos. *Feliz 1958! O ano que não devia terminar*. Rio de Janeiro, Editora Record, 1997.
SEBE, José Carlos. *Carnaval, carnavais*. São Paulo, Editora Ática, 1986.
SILVA, Hélio. *1922, sangue nas areias de Copacabana*. Rio de Janeiro, Civilização Brasileira, 1964.
SUED. Ibrahim. *20 anos de caviar*. Rio de Janeiro, Bloch Editores, 1972.
VELHO, Gilberto. *A utopia urbana: um estudo de antropologia social*. Rio de Janeiro, Zahar, 1973.
VIEIRA, João Luiz. *A chanchada e o cinema carioca (1930-1955)*. In: História do cinema brasileiro. São Paulo, Art, 1987.
WINTERS, Nancy. *Man Flies – The Story of Alberto Santos Dumont, Master of the Balloon*. London, Bloomsbury Publishing, 1997.
WÜNSCH, Fery. *Memórias de um maître hotel*. Rio de Janeiro, Fun Book Editors, 1983.

Periodicals

Newspapers
A Noite
Correio da Manhã
Folha de S. Paulo
Jornal do Brasil
Jornal do Commércio
O Estado de S. Paulo
O Globo
O Jornal
O Malho
O Paiz
Última Hora

Magazines
Beira-Mar
Cadernos do Terceiro Mundo
Careta
Chuvisco
Fon-Fon
Manchete
O Copacabana
O Cruzeiro
O Mundo Ilustrado
Revista da Semana
Rio Magazine
Sombra
Veja
Vozes

Photographic Credits

Photographs are identified from left to right, top to bottom.

Carmélia Alves Collection
pp. 71b, 117a.

Copacabana Palace Archive
pp. 1, 27b (Augusto Malta), 31a, b, 32a, b, c, 33 (Augusto Malta), 34a, b (reproduction by César Barreto), 35, 37 (Augusto Malta), 44, 49b, c, d, 54a, b, c, f, 55a (*O Copacabana*, reproduction by César Barreto), b (*Rio Magazine*, reproduction by César Barreto), 56c, d (*Rio Magazine*, reproduction by César Barreto), e (*Rio Magazine*, reproduction by César Barreto), f (*Rio Magazine*, reproduction by César Barreto), 57b, 58b (*O Copacabana*, reproduction by César Barreto), 60 (*Rio Magazine*, cover by Carlos Thiré, reproduction by César Barreto), 61 (*O Copacabana*, reproduction by César Barreto), 63d (reproduction by César Barreto), 64 (*Rio Magazine*, reproduction by César Barreto), 68a, b, c, 69 (reproduction by César Barreto), 70a (reproduction by César Barreto), 72c (*O Copacabana*, reproduction by César Barreto), d (reproduction by César Barreto), 73a, b (*Rio Magazine*, reproduction by César Barreto), 74a, 75a (*Rio Magazine*, reproduction by César Barreto), b (Olney Krüse), 76a (*O Copacabana*, reproduction by César Barreto), b, 78a (*O Copacabana*, reproduction by César Barreto), b (*O Copacabana*, reproduction by César Barreto), 79b (*O Copacabana*, reproduction by César Barreto), c (*O Copacabana*, reproduction by César Barreto), 80-83, 86a (reproduction by César Barreto), b, 89, 92, 93 (*O Copacabana*, reproduction by César Barreto), 95 (*Rio Magazine*, cover by Michel Burton, reproduction by César Barreto), 98 (*Rio Magazine*, reproduction by César Barreto), 100, 106, 108, 109b, 111 (*O Cruzeiro*, reproduction by César Barreto), 112 (*O Cruzeiro*, reproduction by César Barreto), 113, 114a (*O Cruzeiro*, reproduction by César Barreto), c (*O Copacabana*, reproduction by César Barreto), d (*O Cruzeiro*, reproduction by César Barreto), 115a (reproduction by César Barreto), b (*O Copacabana*, reproduction by César Barreto), c (*O Copacabana*, reproduction by César Barreto), 117b (*Rio Magazine*, reproduction by César Barreto), c (*O Copacabana*, reproduction by César Barreto), 118a (*O Copacabana*, reproduction by César Barreto), b (reproduction by César Barreto), 123a (*O Copacabana*, reproduction by César Barreto), b (*O Copacabana*, reproduction by César Barreto), 124a (*O Copacabana*, reproduction by César Barreto), 125c, 126b, 129b (*O Cruzeiro*, reproduction by César Barreto), c (*O Cruzeiro*, reproduction by César Barreto), d (*O Cruzeiro*, reproduction by César Barreto), e (*O Cruzeiro*, reproduction by César Barreto), 134c (*Sombra* magazine, reproduction by César Barreto), d (*Rio Magazine*, cover by Martin, reproduction by César Barreto), 135a, b (reproduction by César Barreto), c (reproduction by César Barreto), 142, 143a (*Rio Magazine*, reproduction by César Barreto), b, 144, 145b, 147 (*O Cruzeiro*, reproduction by César Barreto), 149, 154b (reproduction by César Barreto), 156 (reproduction by César Barreto), 170a, b.

José Eduardo Guinle Collection
p. 56a.

Murilo and Letícia Neri Collection
pp. 57d, 63c.

Otávio Guinle Filho Collection
pp. 31c, 74b.

Sandra Bernhardt Collection
p. 77c.

Jornal do Brasil Archive
pp. 141a, b (photo by Evandro), 145a (photo by Evandro), 146b (photo by Teixeira), 148 (photo by A. Veiga), 163b, 168a (photo by Isabela Kassow), b (photo by Samuel Martins).

O Globo Archive
p. 137.

General Archive of the City of Rio de Janeiro
pp. 28a (*Paratodos* magazine), 40a, 52 (Hugo), 94.

National Archive
pp. 23b, 24c (Rodrigues and Co.), 25b, 26 (Rodrigues and Co.), 27a (Lopes), 29b (Annunciato), 30b, 51.

National Library
pp. 31d, 36, 42 (*O Jornal*), 53b (*Beira-Mar*), c (*Beira-Mar*), d (*Beira-Mar*), 57c (*O Cruzeiro*), 58c (*O Cruzeiro*), 62b (*O Cruzeiro*), 79a (*O Cruzeiro*), 133a (*O Cruzeiro*), 134a (*O Cruzeiro*), 135d (*O Cruzeiro*).

Cedoc/Funarte
pp. 23a, c, 40b (*Ilustração Brasileira* magazine), 41, 56b, 57a, e, 59 (*Cinearte*), 62a, c, 63a, b, 107, 119, 121, 122, 123c, d, e, 124b, 125b (*A Cena Muda*).

MAM Cinemateca, RJ
pp. 65, 90, 127b, 136d, 139a.

Manchete
pp. 47 (reproduced from *Fon-Fon* magazine), 58a, 70b, 71a, 72a, b, 75b, 77, 88, 105b, 110, 114b, 127a, 128, 138, 140, 146a, 169, 170c.

Museum of Sound and Image
pp. 24a (Augusto Malta), b (Augusto Malta), 25a (Augusto Malta), 28b (Augusto Malta), 30a, 43a (Almirante Collection), b (Almirante Collection), 49a (Augusto Malta), 53a (Guilherme Santos Collection), 133b.

Revista da Semana
p. 46a.

Sergio Pagano
pp. 3, 5, 6, 7, 8, 10, 12-20, 38, 43c, 48, 66, 84, 96, 98b, 104, 116, 120, 130, 150-152, 154a, 155, 157-162, 163a, 164-167, 171-175.

Dados Internacionais de Catalogação na Publicação
(CIP) (Câmara Brasileira do Livro, SP, Brasil)

Boechat, Ricardo
Copacabana Palace : the hotel and its history / by Ricardo Boechat. -- São Paulo : DBA Artes Gráficas, 1999

ISBN 85- 7234-146-3 (DBA)
ISBN 85- 06-03041-2 (Melhoramentos)

1. Copacabana Palace (Hotel), RJ - História
2. Rio de Janeiro - História I. Título

99-0863 CDD- 647.948153

Índices para catálogo sistemático:

1. Copacabana Palace : Hotel : Rio de Janeiro :
Cidade : História 647.948153

Printed in Brazil
DBA Dórea Books and Art
Al. Franca 1185, cj. 31/32, cep 01422-010, São Paulo, SP, Brasil
Tel.: (011) 852 1643 Fax: (011) 280 3361
e-mail: dbabooks@uol.com.br

Companhia Melhoramentos de São Paulo
Atendimento ao consumidor
Caixa Postal 2547 cep 01065 970 São Paulo